Wittgenstein

Wittgenstein

Avrum Stroll

ONEWORLD PHILOSOPHERS

ONEWORLD
OXFORD

WITTGENSTEIN

Oneworld Publications
(Sales and Editorial)
185 Banbury Road
Oxford OX2 7AR
England
www.oneworld-publications.com

© Avrum Stroll 2002

ISBN 1–85168–293–7

Cover design by the Bridgewater Book Company
Cover image © Hulton Archive
Typeset by Saxon Graphics Ltd, Derby, UK
Printed and bound by Clays Ltd, St Ives plc

For Mary

Contents

Acknowledgments

Wittgenstein describes his *Philosophical Investigations* as sketches of landscapes. Given the richness of content of that work, plus its diffuse style, one who writes about Wittgenstein can in no way capture the full range of his thought in any sort of detail. The book that follows is thus also a sketch. So what you will be reading is a sketch of sketches.

Even this vignette would not have been possible without the assistance of many persons who read various versions of the manuscript. I found their comments constructive and helpful. My sincere thanks thus go to Zeno Vendler, Norman Roberson, Pina Pasquantonio, Michael Hersch, Mel Thompson and Daniele Moyal-Sharrock. But above all, I wish to express my deep appreciation to my wife, Mary, who took time away from her own researches into twelfth-century papal politics to scrutinize what I had written. Her comments about organization and style were invaluable. For that, and for other reasons of course, I dedicate this work to her.

Chapter One

The greatest modern philosopher

Wittgenstein's originality

The word 'genius' is frequently applied to mathematicians, scientists, artists, and musicians, but rarely to philosophers. However, there is a notable exception: Ludwig Wittgenstein. Echoing others, Bertrand Russell described him as 'perhaps the most perfect example I have ever known of genius as traditionally conceived, passionate, profound, intense, and dominating.' In a memorable phrase Wittgenstein once wrote: 'Uttering a word is like striking a note on the keyboard of the imagination' (*Philosophical Investigations*, 6). No other twentieth-century philosopher has uttered so many words that struck the keyboard of the imagination. That he was a genius is beyond serious doubt. Because of the originality and depth of his thought, he is widely regarded as the greatest modern philosopher.

Since his death at the age of sixty-two on 29 April 1951, a vast number of articles, monographs, essays, commentaries, and books, have been devoted to his life, personality, and work. Some researchers estimate the number of such items to be more than 7000. Not all of these are technical pieces. There are biographies, plays, a novel, a television drama, and even a video for children in which he is depicted as a computer. Even outside of philosophy he has become a legend. Today his ideas are discussed in anthropology, literature, sociology, psychology, and linguistics. No other twentieth-century philosopher has been the focus of such intense scholarly concentration.

Given this vast outpouring of materials it is sensible to ask: Why do we need another book – the one you are now reading – on Wittgenstein? There are at least two answers to the question. Both are somewhat lengthy. Here is the first. It deals with the need to update and extend the scope of existing commentaries. During his lifetime, Wittgenstein published only two things: a book – the *Tractatus Logico-Philosophicus* in 1922, and a short essay on logical form in 1929. In the twenty-two remaining years of his life, he continued to write incessantly. After his death his executors discovered an enormous legacy of unpublished writings. The amount of material, most of which is still being edited, is estimated to consist of about ninety-five volumes, some of which are non-philosophical, some of which are differing versions of the same works, but most of which are new. The first document to be issued was *Philosophical Investigations*, which appeared in 1953. This is generally regarded as Wittgenstein's masterpiece. Since the *Investigations* another twenty or so volumes have been released, some of them only recently. Exegetes are just now beginning to explore these materials. Most existing studies do not deal with these works. They tend to stop with the *Investigations*. David Pears's *The False Prison* (1987) and P. M. S. Hacker's *Wittgenstein's Place in Twentieth-Century Analytic Philosophy* (1996) exemplify the point. Both are superb books yet they focus entirely on the *Tractatus* and the *Investigations*. A need to update and extend the coverage of the existing scholarship is thus mandatory. This is what I will do in this study. It will deal with Wittgenstein's latest contributions in a way that no other general work does, and this constitutes one justification for writing it.

The second answer is closely related to the first. It provides a new picture of Wittgenstein's intellectual development. Almost all scholars divide Wittgenstein's career into two phases. In their view the first is the time span between 1911 and 1922, and the second is the period from 1929 until his death in 1951. The former begins when he came to Cambridge University to study logic with Bertrand Russell and ends with the publication of the *Tractatus*. That initial stage was interrupted by the outbreak of the First World War in 1914. An Austrian patriot, Wittgenstein immediately left Cambridge and joined the Austrian army. During the war he fought with distinction. In the declining days of the conflict he was captured by the Italians and spent a year in a prison camp near Monte Cassino. During the war he finished writing the *Tractatus* and while in captivity arranged to send the manuscript to Russell who was eventually instrumental in having it published. Thinking that in this work he had solved all the major problems of philosophy, he spent the next decade as an elementary school teacher in Lower Austria and as a self-proclaimed architect, designing a house in Vienna for his sister (Margarete Stonborough) that has since become a national monument.

The second phase begins when he decided to resume his philosophical career. He returned to Cambridge as a graduate student in 1929. Intellectually, this is his most creative period. Much, though not all, of it was spent in England. It was during this 'second phase' that his philosophical ideas changed radically, being based on a new method he invented for dealing with philosophical problems (see Chapter 3). The commentators generally describe this segment as 'the later philosophy of Wittgenstein.' But after Part I of the *Investigations* was completed (probably in 1945), Wittgenstein's philosophical explorations continued unabated and reached new heights. *On Certainty* was his last work. The final seven entries were inserted into the manuscript only two days before his death. A number of scholars now believe that *On Certainty* goes beyond anything contained in either the *Tractatus* or the *Investigations*. They thus see a post-*Investigations* stage in his philosophical development. Daniele Moyal-Sharrock has coined the phrase 'The Third Wittgenstein' to describe his final writings.

The most eminent philosophers of the past have had one significant idea. This is true of Plato, Aristotle, St. Augustine, Descartes, Spinoza, Locke, Berkeley, Hume and Kant. It is also true of many of the best philosophers of the twentieth century: Frege, Russell, Carnap, Ryle, and Quine, for instance. But Wittgenstein stands alone in having had three great ideas: they are found in the *Tractatus*, the *Investigations*, and *On Certainty*, respectively. Indeed, if we turn from philosophy to other creative endeavors of the highest order, it is difficult to find anyone other than Wittgenstein who has had three distinct and important ideas. Consider composers, for example. Bach's polyphonic technique was already set when he was twenty and it never changed throughout his long career. Mozart's style remained essentially the same from beginning to end. One can say comparable things about Schubert, Brahms and Berlioz. In contrast, Beethoven's career had two distinct periods. His early compositions were very much like those of Haydn and Mozart; but by the end of his life his late quartets and piano sonatas soared beyond anything that he, or indeed any other composer, had previously accomplished. Wittgenstein's intellectual growth is thus remarkable. There are huge differences between his early ideas and those of the *Investigations*, and huge differences between those of the *Investigations* and those of *On Certainty*. In agreement with Daniele Moyal-Sharrock, I will emphasize these three phases of his philosophical development in this book. Such an emphasis constitutes a second justification for writing it.

Many scholars have pointed out the revolutionary nature of Wittgenstein's ideas. In a brief biographical sketch, G. H. von Wright, a distinguished Finnish scholar and philosopher, has expressed this point of view as eloquently as anyone. Here is how he states the matter:

> The young Wittgenstein had learned from Frege and Russell. His problems were in part theirs. The later Wittgenstein, in my view, has no ancestors in the history of thought. His work signals a radical departure from previously existing paths of philosophy.

In a footnote, von Wright expands this remark:

> I have seen this statement, and the one preceding it, contested. But I think they are substantially correct and also important. The *Tractatus* belongs in a definite tradition in European philosophy, extending back beyond Frege and Russell at least to Leibniz. Wittgenstein's so called 'later philosophy', as I see it, is quite different. Its *spirit* is unlike

anything I know in Western thought and in many ways opposed to aims and methods in traditional philosophy. This is not incompatible with the fact – about which more is known now than when this essay was first published – that many of Wittgenstein's later ideas have *seeds* in works which he had read and conversations he had with others. It is interesting to note what Wittgenstein himself says about this in *Vermischte Bemerkungen* (*Culture and Value*) especially pp. 18ff and 36. In the latter place he says: 'I believe my originality (if that is the right word) is an originality belonging to the soil rather than to the seed. (Perhaps I have no seed of my own.) Sow a seed in my soil and it will grow differently than it would in any other soil.'

In a later passage von Wright states, 'As late as two days before his death he wrote down thoughts that are equal to the best he produced.' In this passage Wright is indirectly referring to *On Certainty*. The quotation supports Moyal-Sharrock's thesis that Wittgenstein's final writings mark a third stage in his philosophical development.

Wittgenstein says that his originality belongs to the soil rather than to the seed. What is the difference between these two kinds of originality? The remark is eye-stopping and goes to the heart of what makes the later Wittgenstein different from anyone else in Western philosophy. A full answer is possible only after we have explored his three great ideas. But one can get a preliminary sense of his orientation by contrasting his philosophy with a flow of thought inherited from the Greeks. The later Wittgenstein stands at the end and outside of that tradition and can be thought of as turning it on its head. The tradition sees the ordinary person as confused and in need of philosophical therapy. Socrates is the paradigmatic philosopher on this view. He walked around Athens questioning his fellow citizens and quickly exposed the shallowness and inconsistencies of their thinking about fundamental issues. For Wittgenstein the emphasis is in the other direction. It is philosophers like Socrates and his successors who 'tend to cast up a dust and then complain they cannot see' and who need help. Therefore in order to explain why his 'soil' is different from anyone else's, let us look briefly at the tradition we have inherited from the Greeks, and then contrast Wittgenstein's approach with it. We shall find that what is true of the earliest of Greek thinkers, Thales, is generally true of his successors up to the later Wittgenstein.

Textbooks give Thales' dates as 625–546 B.C., usually adding that these figures are only approximate. Thales was famous among his countrymen as an intellectual prodigy. He was a legislator, a mathematician, an astronomer (who predicted an eclipse of the sun in 585 B.C.) and of course a speculative thinker. Some of what is known about him comes from the historian Herodotus, who was born about fifty years after Thales died, and some from a still later author, Aristotle. In his *Metaphysics*, Aristotle wrote an account of his philosophical predecessors, beginning with Thales. He says that Thales believed that the fundamental stuff of reality was water. As Aristotle puts it, Thales saw that the 'nourishment of all things is moist, and that warmth itself is generated from moisture and persists in it; and also that the seeds of all things are of a moist nature,' and concluded that 'water is the first principle' of nature. As an inhabitant of a coastal city in Asia Minor, Thales was aware of the enormous stretch of water composing the Mediterranean Sea. It is also believed that he visited Egypt and saw the vast outpouring of water that flows into the Nile basin. In saying that the nourishment of all things is moist, he attempted to demonstrate that a simple theory will reveal a basic connection between seemingly diverse natural objects, processes and events – plants, soil, ice, and animals. The theory was designed to uncover the common characteristic (essence) that all things possess. His argument was that water was this characteristic.

Thales and his successors in the Greek tradition engaged in speculations about a spectrum of topics, ranging from moral and theological considerations to those that today we would call scientific. In each case they were attempting to show that certain basic principles explain a wide range of phenomena. They were interested in such questions as: What is the fundamental nature of reality? Is there some primal stuff from which all diversity emerges? What remains constant when something changes? What is the difference between mind and matter? Where did the universe come from? Is the sun a rock? Is it possible to obtain knowledge/certainty about nature? Is there any meaning or purpose in life and if so what is it? What is the nature of the good life for man? and so forth. Their ways of dealing with such questions emphasized reason, rather than experiment. They presupposed that rational inquiry would by itself answer all such questions. It was only two thousand years later that Galileo began a new tradition in which it gradually became apparent that reason would have to be supplemented by experiment in order to obtain an accurate picture of the workings of nature.

As a result of this new understanding, inquiries that had originally been treated as part of philosophy gradually separated themselves from the parent discipline. Even as late as the seventeenth century, the physicist Isaac Newton described himself as a 'natural philosopher.' But as a consequence of his work, physics soon became an autonomous discipline. In this respect, it was rapidly followed by chemistry and biology, and then in the twentieth century by psychology, anthropology, sociology, political science and linguistics.

Nonetheless, philosophy managed to survive, but not without feeling the effects of these defections. On the one hand, it recognized that the kinds of experimental/theoretical investigations that science conducted were of a different order from anything philosophers could or should do. There was thus a growing and explicit recognition that scientific exploration differed in kind from philosophical inquiry. Yet this acknowledgment did not mean that there were no commonalities among these differing activities. Both were committed to exploring, understanding, and thus ultimately to explaining the inanimate and animate aspects of the world, and both were committed to rigor in argumentation, to the same canons of evidence and proof, and to the use of reason and logic in arriving at knowledge and truth. The tradition thus envisioned its activities as running parallel to those of science. We might say that it saw itself as a kind of non-experimental science. In arguing that water was the basic stuff of reality, Thales was presupposing this parallelism and the tradition followed him in accepting its principles as central to philosophical inquiry.

These are sensible and compelling notions and it is hard to imagine that they could seriously be challenged by anyone whose commitment is to rational inquiry. Yet, in his later writings Wittgenstein explicitly disavowed the assumption that philosophy is and should be a kind of parallel science. In his view theory building by philosophers imposed a restricted conceptual scheme on a complex world and in so doing misrepresented it. Accordingly, the philosophical urge for a deeper explanation led not to understanding but to paradox and confusion. A new conception of the nature and purpose of philosophy was thus required. In Wittgenstein's later writings this new approach rests on a method he invented for dealing with philosophical problems. Wittgenstein does not talk much about the method but applies it in a detailed way, thus showing by his practice how certain seemingly obdurate philosophical issues can be resolved. His assumption seems to be that the reader will pick up the method by seeing it in operation. The outcome of his work is to challenge the entire tradition that has come down to us from Thales. In a series of lectures he gave in 1939 on the foundations of mathematics, he said about his method:

> You might, to be very misleading, call this investigation an investigation into the meaning of certain words. But this is apt to lead to misunderstandings.
>
> The investigation is to draw your attention to facts you know quite as well as I, but which you have forgotten, or at least which are not immediately in your field of vision. They will all be quite trivial facts. I won't say anything which anyone can dispute. Or if anyone does dispute it, I will let that point drop and pass on to say something else.

Somewhat later he was to write:

> Philosophy simply puts everything before us, and neither explains nor deduces anything. Since everything lies open to view there is nothing to explain. For what is hidden, for example, is of no interest to us.
>
> One might also give the name 'philosophy' to what is possible before all new discoveries and inventions ... The work of the philosopher consists in assembling reminders for a particular purpose ... If one tried to advance theses in philosophy, it would never be possible to debate them, because everyone would agree to them. (*Philosophical Investigations*, 126–128)

As these quotations make plain, Wittgenstein is denying that one of philosophy's fundamental purposes is to explain anything. Indeed, he differs from the tradition and from science in stating that nothing needs to be explained *because nothing is hidden.* He means, of course, that nothing is hidden from philosophy – but that is just the difference between philosophy and science. As he says in the *Investigations,* 'We want to *understand* something that is already in plain view. For *this* is what we seem in some sense not to understand.' This is why 'one might give the name "philosophy" to what is possible before new discoveries and inventions,' and why the work of the philosopher 'consists in assembling reminders for a particular purpose.' Elsewhere he rejects the idea that philosophy should develop theories. As he says, 'description should replace explanation,' and by an explanation he means a theory. It is clear we are dealing with a revolutionary thinker here. To make these non-traditional conceptions plausible, indeed even to explain what they are, is the main purpose of this book and Chapters 2–4 will be dedicated to this endeavor. But before turning to that task I shall devote the rest of the chapter to his remarkable life and personality.

The young Wittgenstein and familial influence

Even though Wittgenstein's thought has spilled beyond the boundaries of philosophy into other academic domains, he is not the kind of philosopher whose work is known to the general public. In this respect he differs from Bertrand Russell, for instance, who became famous for opposing Britain's involvement in the First World War and who, along with Albert Einstein and Linus Pauling, protested against the development and deployment of nuclear weapons after the Second World War. There is a wonderful story in illustration of this point that involves the English philosopher, G. E. Moore. In 1951 Moore was awarded the Order of Merit, the highest honor that a man of letters could receive in the British Empire. The presentation was made by King George VI, who afterwards spoke with Moore for a short period and then arose, indicating that the ceremony was at an end. Moore returned to the taxicab where his wife was waiting and leaning over excitedly said: 'Do you know that the king has never heard of Wittgenstein!' It is probably true that the general reader, like the king, has never heard of Wittgenstein and it is even more probable that he or she has never read anything written by him. Nonetheless, Wittgenstein had a remarkable personality and led an interesting life. Russell's four words capture much of the man: he was *passionate, profound, intense,* and *dominating.* To these we can also add that he was *guilt ridden, insecure,* and *doubtful* of his own abilities. He thus had the kind of personality that most of us think geniuses should have. And the kind of life he led was in perfect conformity with that personality. In nearly every way it deviated from the ordinary. It is thus not remarkable that there should be a spate of biographies about him.

His character and career were to a considerable extent determined by the unusual family in which he was reared. Wittgenstein was the youngest of eight children. Hermine, the eldest, was fifteen years older than Ludwig. Each parent and each sibling was a strong personality and as a group they were close-knit. The impact they made on Ludwig was profound and resonated throughout his life. A simple example: three of his four brothers committed suicide, and Ludwig on several occasions contemplated doing so as well. His brother Rudolf was driven to this action by homosexual guilt. I have mentioned that Wittgenstein was also guilt ridden. He was so for many reasons, but his homosexual impulses and practices were important among them (I shall have more to say about this later). The sisters, by way of contrast, were less emotional and played a stabilizing role in Wittgenstein's life. This was especially true of Hermine, who consoled him in moments of depression and stress.

Moreover, the family was incredibly wealthy. Wittgenstein's father, Karl, was an industrialist whose success in the iron and steel industry made him one of the richest men in Europe. In 1898, having accumulated a fortune, he decided to retire from business. But in a prescient move he transferred all of his securities into US equities. This had the benefit of protecting the family against the wild inflation in Austria and Germany that followed the First World War. Each of the children was to inherit a fortune. But Ludwig followed a wholly different course from the others. After returning from the war in 1919 he decided to dispose of his entire inheritance and insisted that it should be transferred to his sisters Helene and Hermine and to his brother Paul. He arranged with the family's monetary adviser to make sure that none of these funds would be returned to him in any shape or form. The accountant reluctantly helped Wittgenstein to commit a less fatal form of suicide, namely 'financial suicide.' From then on his life was almost monk-like in its austerity. When Frank Ramsey visited Wittgenstein in Lower Austria, where he was teaching in 1923, Ramsey described his situation in these words: 'He is very poor, at least he lives very economically. He has one tiny room whitewashed, containing a bed, washstand, small table, and one hard chair and that is all there is room for. His evening meal which I shared last night is rather unpleasant coarse bread, butter and cocoa.' Despite the efforts of his siblings to subvert his desire for financial self-destruction, Wittgenstein refused to accept any assistance from them. Norman Malcolm tells an amusing story in this connection. When Wittgenstein visited Malcolm at Cornell in 1949, the Malcolms offered to make him an elegant dinner. Thanking them, he refused, stating that he preferred something simple. He then added that he liked food but it had to be the same thing for every meal.

Wittgenstein's mother, Leopoldine, was a pianist with talents at the professional level. His brother Hans was a musical prodigy who at the age of four could play the piano and violin and compose original music. Another brother, Paul, was a touring pianist who lost his right arm in the First World War. He managed to have a distinguished subsequent career, playing special compositions for the left hand alone, written for him by Ravel and Scriabin. The three sisters all had strong artistic interests. Margarete ('Gretl'), close in age to Ludwig, was considered the avante-garde intellectual of the family. She admired the philosophy of Schopenhauer, and was a revolutionary spirit prepared to entertain new developments in the arts, literature and science. She was also an early supporter of Sigmund Freud and was psychoanalyzed by him. She introduced Ludwig to the work of Karl Kraus, a witty, Voltaire-like journalist who was the rage among Viennese intellectuals for his stinging criticisms of the policies of the decaying Austro-Hungarian empire. Margarete agreed with Kraus and her attitudes affected the young Ludwig. Some resonances of Schopenhauerian influences are to be found in the mystical later sections of the *Tractatus*. The third sister, Helene, was also an accomplished pianist. She had four children and eight grandchildren. When the Nazis occupied Austria she was at first declared to be a Jew and thus subject to the severe racial laws they imposed. But after a complicated series of negotiations in which Ludwig participated, and in which a portion of the family fortune was given to the Nazis, she and her family were declared not to be Jews, or even to be of mixed blood, and accordingly she was able to survive the Nazi occupation. Hermine was especially close to Ludwig and stood in an almost maternal relationship to him. Her written recollections provide a revealing psychological portrait of Ludwig. After Ludwig's disavowal of the fortune left to him by his father, Hermine wrote that 'it is not easy to have a saint for a brother, and I would rather have a happy person for a brother than an unhappy saint.'

Wittgenstein was reared in an environment of wealth and culture that is rare today. Among the friends the family entertained were the musicians Johannes Brahms, Joseph Joachim, and Gustav Mahler, and various writers, artists and architects, such as Gustav Klimt and Adolf Loos. Klimt's portrait of Margarete is a modern classic, and Loos directly influenced the architect Paul Engelmann, who designed her house. The Wittgenstein establishment was thus a cultural center in *fin-de-siècle* Vienna. Wittgenstein was to absorb these influences in ways that especially affected his personal life but, paradoxically enough, hardly his philosophy at all. All of his most important works deal with technical issues and have little cultural relevance. It is true that in *Culture and Value*, *Lectures on Aesthetics*, *Conversations on Freud* and other short essays he deals with such matters, but they are all minor pieces compared with his major contributions.

Ludwig and Margarete were the least gifted musically in the family. Ludwig only learned to play an instrument (the clarinet) when he was in his early thirties as part of his teaching duties in Lower Austria. His interests as a child and as a young man lay in technical and mechanical activities, such as working with lathes and various tools and instruments. When he was seventeen his parents decided that he should become an engineer and he spent two years in a vocational school in Berlin. After graduating he decided to become an aeronautical engineer, and so in 1908 at the age of nine-teen he enrolled as a research student at the University of Manchester. His first experiments concerned the design of kites but eventually he became interested in the design of propellers and airplane engines. Plans still exist for some of his designs and show an inventive mind at at work. During his stay in Manchester a friend introduced him to Bertrand Russell's *Principles of Mathematics*, first published in 1903. Wittgenstein was captivated by its argument. In this work Russell advanced what was later to be called 'the logistic thesis.' This is the contention that mathematics is a branch of logic.

When he began this treatise, Russell did not know that Gottlob Frege (1848–1925) had attempted a similar demonstration in his *Begriffschrift* of 1879. Frege is generally regarded as the inventor of mathematical logic, but his work was unknown even to his German contemporaries. It was Russell who first brought his contributions to the attention of the scholarly world. The *Principles of Mathematics* was virtually finished before Russell became acquainted with Frege's writings. The *Principles of Mathematics* did not carry out the demonstration but rather suggested how it might be done. Russell and his collaborator, Alfred North Whitehead, were in fact to complete the task in their magisterial three-volume work, *Principia Mathematica*, which took about ten years to write and whose third volume was published in 1913. Despite this great achievement there is considerable dispute about whether they were successful or not. Their approach depended on principles that subsequent logicians have questioned, such as the Axiom of Reducibility and the Axiom of Infinity. They also employed notions that are now recognized to belong to what is called 'set theory.' Sets are collections of objects, and are abstractions having a peculiar status, being neither physical nor concrete. Set theory is thus gener-ally distinguished from logic in a narrow sense of the term, i.e., as whatever concerns only rules for propositional connectives, quanti-fiers and nonspecific terms for individuals and predicates.

Furthermore, *Principia* employed the concept of identity (denoted by the symbol '='). Though most logicians have assumed that it is part of logic in a narrow sense, even this is controversial. Accordingly, Whitehead and Russell's attempt to prove the logistic thesis has been widely challenged and many logicians maintain that the thesis has not yet been proven. Nonetheless, their endeavor was a creation of the highest importance and has had a lasting effect on subsequent work in logic and some parts of mathematics. It totally eclipsed scholastic logic, a theory of inference which had existed since the time of Aristotle. This would have astounded Immanuel Kant, who at the end of the eighteenth century stated that logic was complete and beyond further development. In *Principia* the whole of scholastic logic occupies a few paragraphs in a work consisting of about fifteen hundred pages.

Their approach consisted in showing that what are called 'Peano's Postulates' could be derived wholly within their system. The postulates were formulated by the Italian mathematician Giuseppe Peano in 1895, and are the basis of the natural number series. Natural numbers, such as the sequence 1, 2, 3 ... ... n are distinguished from integers which not only include the natural numbers, but also negative numbers, such as $^-1$, $^-2$, $^-3$ ... ... $-n$. The two number systems have different logical bases, the integers being derived via 'upper and lower bounds,' or 'Dedekind cuts,' developed by the German mathematician Richard Dedekind (1831–1916), and the natural numbers from Peano's postulates. In *Principia Mathematica*, Russell and Whitehead were able to derive Peano's five postulates, showing them to be formulable in wholly logical terms. This entailed that mathematics was indeed a branch of logic and that logic was the more fundamental of the two disciplines. Here are the postulates:

1. Zero is a number.
2. The successor of any number is a number.
3. No two numbers have the same successor.
4. Zero is not the successor of any number.
5. If any property is possessed by zero, and also by the successor of any number having that property, then all numbers have that property.

The last of these is the principle of mathematical induction.

After the publication of *Begriffschrift* Frege continued to work at the logistic thesis and found, as Russell was to do later, that he had a monumental task on his hands. Volume 1 of his *Grundgesetze der Arithmetik* (*Fundamental Laws of Arithmetic*) was published in 1893 and a second volume in 1903. Russell had discovered the first volume of *Grundgesetze* just as he was completing the *Principles of Mathematics*. He realized that Frege's system was susceptible to a paradox that showed its foundations to be inconsistent. This difficulty, called 'Russell's paradox,' has become famous in the history of philosophy. In attempting to prove the logistic thesis, Frege had made use of the concept of a class and gave this notion a particular interpretation, namely that it was the *Bedeutung* or extension of a concept. Thus, the concept *dog* refers to the class of canines, and the concept *aardvark* to the class of aardvarks, and so forth. Russell pointed out that the principle that each concept denotes a class leads to a contradiction.

This follows from the fact that there are some classes that are members of themselves and some that are not. The class of all classes is itself a class, and therefore is a member of itself; but the class of dogs is not a dog and therefore is not a member of itself. It is thus possible to form a class, K, which is the class of all classes that are not members of themselves. And now a key question: Is K a member of itself? Either it is or it is not. Either answer leads to a contradiction. The basic problem can be explained in ordinary English. Let us assume that there is a village in which there is a barber who shaves all those and only those who do not shave themselves. The words 'all' and 'only' are key to the paradox. We can now ask: Who shaves the barber? Either he shaves or he does not shave. If he shaves himself, he shaves at least one person who shaves himself and accordingly does not shave *only* those who do not shave themselves. If he does not shave himself, then another must shave him, and accordingly he does not shave *all* those who do not shave themselves. It follows from the paradox that the fundamental principle of Fregean logic that describes a relationship between concepts and classes leads to a contradiction. Therefore, it cannot be used as a foundation for the reduction of mathematics to logic.

After discovering this difficulty, Russell wrote Frege who attempted to emend the second volume of *Grundgesetze* before its publication; but his rectification failed. The task of demonstrating the logistic thesis thus fell on Russell and Whitehead. The period between 1879 and 1913 was one of the most inventive and exciting periods in the history of philosophy. Wittgenstein was caught up in these challenging developments and decided that when he graduated from Manchester he should abandon engineering in favor of philosophy. In 1911 he went to Frege to discuss his future. Frege urged him to go to England to study with Russell, then, in Frege's view, the premier figure in logic. And Wittgenstein followed his advice.

Wittgenstein and Russell, 1911–1914

Wittgenstein was twenty-one when in 1911 he began to work with Russell. For about three years he was an undergraduate at Cambridge and Russell was his supervisor. When they first met Wittgenstein was a neophyte in logic. By the end of Wittgenstein's first year, Russell stated that he had nothing more to teach him and told Hermine that 'we expect the next big step in philosophy to be taken by your brother.' Russell was right on both counts. But even he did not anticipate how rapidly his prediction would come true. In 1918 Russell gave a series of lectures in London that were motivated by the principle that mathematical logic has significant philosophical implications. He called the resulting doctrine 'Logical Atomism.' What is particularly interesting is that Russell credited Wittgenstein with having originated this view while Wittgenstein was still his pupil. He begins the published version of the lectures by saying:

> The following is the text of a course of eight lectures delivered in (Gordon Square) London, in the first months of 1918, which are very largely concerned with explaining certain ideas which I learnt from my friend and former pupil Ludwig Wittgenstein. I have had no opportunity of knowing his views since August 1914, and I do not even know whether he is alive or dead. He has therefore no responsibility for what is said in these lectures beyond that of having originally supplied many of the theories contained in them.

In the text, on page 205, there is a virtual duplicate of this comment. There Russell says:

A very great deal of what I am saying in this course of lectures consists of ideas which I derived from my friend Wittgenstein. But I have had no opportunity of knowing how far his ideas have changed since August 1914, nor whether he is alive or dead, so I cannot make anyone but myself responsible for them.

The ideas that Russell is referring to were developed by Wittgenstein in the period 1911–1914, and are precursors to the view we later find in the *Tractatus*. According to Russell, the logical system of *Principia Mathematica* 'implied' – though not in the strict sense of 'imply' – a certain metaphysical world view, and it was this, with his own variations, that Russell named 'Logical Atomism.' Wittgenstein was not to use this term in the *Tractatus* but his early notebooks indicate that Russell's understanding of the main thrust of his thinking before he departed for Austria was correct. Here is how Russell's account begins:

> In the present lectures, I shall try to set forth in a sort of outline, briefly and unsatisfactorily, a kind of logical doctrine which seems to me to result from the philosophy of mathematics – not exactly logi-cally, but what emerges as one reflects: a certain kind of logical doctrine, and on the basis of this a certain kind of metaphysics. The logic which I shall advocate is atomistic, as opposed to the monistic logic of the people who more or less follow Hegel. When I say that my logic is atomistic, I mean that I share the common-sense belief that there are many separate things: I do not regard the apparent multiplicity of the world as consisting merely in phases and unreal divisions of a single indivisible Reality.

This three-year period in which Wittgenstein's genius exploded on the philosophical scene has fascinated intellectual historians. Given the complexity of the new logic, it seems impossible that Wittgenstein could have mastered it in such a short time. Today in almost every American university mathematical logic is taught to hundreds of undergraduates. It is much more advanced than the Russell/Whitehead system. But in its day it was understood only by a handful of specialists. Even in the late 1920s the only logic taught at Oxford was scholastic logic. Though philosophy was a popular subject at Cambridge, Russell's lectures were often attended by only three or four students, and by the occasional colleague, like G. E. Moore. Wittgenstein was present at every session, and indeed became a kind of incubus who would not let any point drop. He dominated the discussions and continued to argue with Russell for hours afterwards. Russell described him as 'my ferocious German.'

During a summer vacation in 1912 Ludwig wrote a paper that Russell decided was far better than anything his English pupils could do. On this basis he encouraged Wittgenstein, even suggesting that he might do *great* work in the future. Wittgenstein's self-doubts about whether philosophy should be his life's work immediately came to an end. As he said to a friend, Russell's enthusiasm proved his salvation. It ended years of loneliness and mental turmoil, years during which he had thought of committing suicide and often felt ashamed that he had not done so. Yet, as Wittgenstein's knowledge of logic deepened, his attitude toward Russell underwent a change. Wittgenstein began to feel that Russell was becoming a popularizer and was no longer interested in fundamental research. Russell in turn found Wittgenstein increasingly patronizing. There were frequently painful moments between them. Once Russell queried: 'Are you thinking about logic or your sins?' Wittgenstein continued to pace back and forth and finally replied: 'Both.' The final months before Wittgenstein left for Austria were especially difficult. Nonetheless, Russell never stopped admiring Wittgenstein's abilities and even in periods of considerable tension felt that Ludwig was the only person he knew who could make real advances in logic.

In part Russell's problem was one of psychological exhaustion. The intensive ten years he had devoted to writing *Principia Mathematica* had taken a terrible toll. In his three-volume autobiography he stated that he had never recovered from the labor required to write this work, and that 'since finishing it I was definitely less capable of dealing with difficult abstractions than I was before.' It should be stressed that the axiomatic system that he and Whitehead had created required that each theorem be constructively proved – a tremendous effort given the size of the project. Some four decades later, when I was a student at Berkeley, the instructor gave the class, as an exercise, the task of constructively proving various theorems in *Principia*. I spent a month grappling with *one* of the propositions in Chapter 20 and finally gave up. Today, using natural deduction, the task would be comparatively simple. But natural deduction was not to be invented until the 1930s so Russell had to use the only techniques then available to him. Though he was only thirty-nine in 1911 he felt that he would never again be able to do ground-breaking work in logic. He was thus looking for somebody who could carry on where he had left off. Once he became aware of Wittgenstein's talent and deep commitment to the subject, he realized that he had found his protégé. Wittgenstein by now had such a command of the material that he was able to show that some of the proofs in *Principia* were flawed. When he pointed these out, Russell's response was to hand him the torch. Russell admitted he did not have the energy to rework the material and told Ludwig that it was now up to him to revise *Principia.*

In 1913 Wittgenstein decided to take the year off and move to Norway to work out his developing ideas. He felt that he could not do creative work in the donnish and stuffy atmosphere of Cambridge. He found a tiny village in which he could isolate himself. It was called Skjolden, and was located in the mountains north of Bergen. There, almost without interruption, he devoted himself to logic. Later he was to say that in Skjolden 'his mind was on fire.' Wittgenstein was simultaneously working on a variety of topics. One of them consisted in trying to develop a method for showing in a mechanical way whether a well-formed string of symbols is a theorem. In this task he was successful and the procedure is now called 'the truth table method.' It works only for the propositional (sentential) calculus, to be sure, but there it works infallibly. It is still taught in courses in elementary logic and can be applied by machines. In a fully worked-out form it appears in the *Tractatus.* Since that work was finished at the end of 1918, Wittgenstein's achievement preceded that of E. L. Post, who published a similar tabular method in 1920. As a decision procedure it is a brilliant creation. Yet it is only one of the many original ideas in the *Tractatus.*

At this time Wittgenstein was also developing a distinction that was to be central to the *Tractatus*, i.e., the difference between saying and showing. He regarded this notion as of the highest importance. He thought, among other things, that it would demonstrate that the Theory of Types was superfluous. The Theory of Types was Russell's solution to the paradox he had originally found in Frege's *Grundgesetze*. It held, in effect, that the paradox about K being the class of all classes that are not members of themselves could be neutralized if K was shown to belong to a different type or order from the propositions about the classes that were subsumed under it. The solution indeed blocked the paradox, but Russell himself realized that it was ad hoc and in the long run would have to be modified or abandoned. But nobody in the following decade had been able to improve on it. In Wittgenstein's opinion he had now done so. In the next chapter I will discuss the distinction as it appears in the *Tractatus*, and in a subsequent chapter why it totally disappears in his later philosophy. It is an original and penetrating concept and yet it has been widely criticized. Whatever evaluation of it we eventually arrive at, the evidence is overwhelming that Wittgenstein's year in Norway had indeed set his mind on fire.

In June of 1914 Wittgenstein left Norway for a brief vacation in Vienna. A month later the First World War broke out, and he enlisted in the Austrian army. It was to be an 'extended vacation.' He was not to resume his affiliation with Cambridge for another fifteen years.

The intervening years, 1919–1929

On 11 November 1918, with the signing of the armistice ending the First World War, the Habsburg Empire ceased to exist. Before the armistice, the Austro-Hungarian Empire included what is presently the Czech Republic, Slovakia, all of Hungary (though historically the ruler of Hungary was always a king and never an emperor), about half of Romania, Yugoslavia, and parts of northern Italy. Even today in Bressanone, just north of Trento, German is the local language rather than Italian. The dissassembling of Austria and the severe reparations demanded in the Versaille Treaty left the country in a shambles. The urban population of Austria basically lived on the relief provided by the United States and Great Britain from 1919 through 1921. For the next seventeen years, until the Anschluss of 1938 by Hitler ended its independent existence, the country went from one political crisis to another. On top of everything else there was endemic inflation. Ludwig was released from his Italian prison camp just when the politico-economic troubles began to gather steam.

It tells us something about his personality that the deteriorating condition of the country seems hardly to have affected him. Like many geniuses, his concentration was upon himself and/or his work. The outside world was peripheral to the mental world he inhabited. Economically, as I pointed out earlier, his family was enormously wealthy thanks to the strategic economic arrangements his father had made two decades earlier. In that ambience there was no scarcity and no need for British or American relief. The turmoil he felt was apolitical. It was internal and personal, and much of it arose from homosexual impulses and actions, about which he felt guilty and at times even suicidal. It is true that the opulence of the Wittgenstein family turned out to be unendurable for him, and this led him to disinherit himself. When he was writing the *Tractatus* he suffered severely, but some of those struggles and discontents arose from conceptual challenges. However, once he had finished the book, he felt that he had solved all philosophical problems. As he now saw it there was nothing left for him to do. He was thirty and at a crossroads. So he cast about for a new career that would be meaningful and at the same time would bring him the kind of mental balance and repose he felt he desperately needed.

He finally decided – to the horror of his family – to become an elementary school teacher. His siblings could not understand how a man whom Russell had declared to be a philosophical genius, and who came from a rich, aristocratic family that was one of the pillars of Austrian culture, could throw his life away teaching ignorant and crude peasant children. And yet that, to their dismay, is what he decided to do. He went to great lengths to make sure that the teaching situation would be arduous – that it would take place in a tiny, rustic, primitive village somewhere. He finally decided on a hamlet called Trattenbach. It is located in hilly country, about midway between Vienna and Graz. Neighboring Kirchberg am Wechsel, whose population cannot be a thousand, seems like a metropolis by comparison. (Kirchberg is where the Austrian Wittgenstein Society holds its annual meetings. It contains a large conference center, a museum devoted to Wittgenstein, and three or four hotels and restaurants.) Trattenbach has a handful of houses and a tiny school. As one might have expected, the combination of Wittgenstein and rustic, unmotivated elementary students was a total mismatch. Within a short time he became disillusioned and in September 1922 moved to a secondary school near Trattenbach. He soon formed a negative impression of the students and teachers there, and quickly sought another position, this time in Puchberg, where Frank Ramsey visited him in 1923. The pattern repeated itself, and so in September 1924 he moved to Otterthal, another tiny village near Trattenbach. His sister Hermine described him as an excellent teacher, and in her recollections wrote:

> I myself had the opportunity of watching Ludwig teach on a number of occasions … It was a marvellous treat for all of us. He did not simply lecture, but tried to lead the boys to the correct solutions by means of questions. On one occasion he had them inventing a steam engine, on another designing a tower on the blackboard, and on yet another depicting moving human figures. The interest which he aroused was enormous. Even the ungifted and usually inattentive among the boys came up with astonishingly good answers, and they were positively climbing over each other in their eagerness to be given a chance to answer or to demonstrate a point.

It was in Otterthal in 1926 that his teaching career came to a sudden end. Like most Austrian schoolmasters he was given to the use of corporal punishment as a way of imposing discipline in the classroom. He once pulled a girl's hair so hard that some of it fell out. But the decisive moment came when in anger he struck an eleven-year-old boy, Josef Haidbauer, causing him to collapse. On seeing this, Wittgenstein panicked. He sent the class home and called a doctor to attend the youngster. The child recovered but because of complaints filed against Wittgenstein, the school administration held a hearing to discuss the case. He was cleared of misconduct but lied about the degree of force he had used. This lie was to haunt him for years and we shall speak about its effect on him below. The outcome of the hearing was that he suddenly and forcefully realized that the life of a schoolmaster was not for him. On 28 April 1926, he departed from Otterthal, and by the summer of that year was back in the family home in Vienna. He was now only three years away from returning to philosophy in Cambridge.

From 1926 to 1928 Wittgenstein assisted the architect Paul Engelmann in designing and building a house for his sister Margarete. Margarete, as I mentioned earlier, was much involved in the intellectual life of Vienna. One of her acquaintances was Moritz Schlick. Schlick was the author of an important book on the philosophy of science, *General Theory of Knowledge* (*Die Allgemeine Erkenntnislehre*) published in 1918. He was also the founder of the Vienna Circle (*Der Wiener Kreis*). This was a group of like-minded intellectuals, mostly scientists and mathematicians, who met regularly and eventually developed a common philosophy they called 'Logical Positivism' or 'Logical Empiricism;' and which was to have an enormous influence on subsequent twentieth-century thought. They were much influenced by the *Tractatus* and by *Principia Mathematica*. They wholeheartedly accepted Russell's thesis that philosophy should be scientific ('scientific' for them meaning 'empirical') and grounded in logic. Schlick had read the *Tractatus* shortly after it was published and regarded it as a work of genius. He tried on a number of occasions, invariably unsuccessfully, to get in touch with Wittgenstein, and even made a trip to Puchberg only to find that Wittgenstein had resigned his teaching post and had returned to Vienna.

In February 1927 Margarete arranged a dinner party so that he could meet her brother. During the course of the evening, Schlick invited Wittgenstein to meet informally with a few members of the Circle to discuss the *Tractatus* and some problems in logic. It turned out to be a small group: Schlick himself, Rudolf Carnap, Friedrich Waismann and Herbert Feigl. By now Carnap had become the intellectual leader of the Circle and he, like Schlick, greatly admired Wittgenstein. Indeed he later wrote in his autobiography that 'Wittgenstein was perhaps the philosopher who, besides Russell and Frege, had the greatest influence on my thinking.' Like most of the members of the Circle he had never met Wittgenstein and was avidly looking forward to the opportunity. In his autobiography he describes what happened.

> Before the first meeting, Schlick admonished us urgently not to start a discussion of the kind to which we were accustomed in the Circle, because Wittgenstein did not want such a thing under any circumstances. We should even be cautious in asking questions, because Wittgenstein was very sensitive and easily disturbed by a direct question. The best approach, Schlick said, would be to let Wittgenstein talk and then ask only very cautiously for the necessary elucidations.

> When I met Wittgenstein, I saw that Schlick's warnings were fully justified. But his behavior was not caused by any arrogance. In general, he was of a sympathetic temperament and very kind; but he was hypersensitive and easily irritated. Whatever he said was always interesting and stimulating, and the way in which he expressed it was often fascinating. His point of view and his attitude toward people and problems, even theoretical problems, were much more similar to those of a creative artist than to a scientist; one might almost say, similar to those of a religious prophet or seer. When he started to formulate his view on some specific problem, we often felt the internal struggle that occurred in him at that very moment, a struggle by which he tried to penetrate from darkness to light under an intensive and painful strain, which was even visible on his most expressive face. When finally, sometimes after a prolonged arduous effort, his answer came forth, his statement stood before us like a newly created piece of art or a divine revelation ... the impression he made on us was as if insight came to him as through a divine inspiration, so that we could not help feeling that any sober rational comment or analysis of it would be a profanation.

> Thus, there was a striking difference between Wittgenstein's attitude toward philosophical problems and that of Schlick and myself. Our attitude toward philosophical problems was not very different from that which scientists have toward their problems. For us the discussion of doubts and objections of others seemed the best way of testing a new idea in the field of philosophy just as much as in the fields of science; Wittgenstein, on the other hand, tolerated no critical examination by others, once the insight had been gained by an act of inspiration ... Earlier when we were reading Wittgenstein's book in the Circle, I had erroneously believed that his attitude toward metaphysics was similar to ours. I had not paid sufficient attention to the statements in his book about the mystical, because his feelings

and thoughts in this area were too divergent from mine ... Even at the times when the contrast in *Weltanschauung* and basic personal attitude became apparent, I found the association with him most interesting, exciting, and rewarding. Therefore, I regretted it when he broke off the contact. From the beginning of 1929 on, Wittgenstein wished to meet only with Schlick and Waismann, no longer with me and Feigl, who had also become acquainted with him in the meantime, let alone with the Circle. Although the difference in our attitudes and personalities expressed itself only on certain occasions, I understood very well that Wittgenstein felt it all the time and, unlike me, was disturbed by it. He said to Schlick that he could talk only with somebody who 'holds his hand.'

As his account makes plain, Carnap was surprised to find that the Wittgenstein he was now talking with did not exactly correspond to the person who had written the *Tractatus* a decade earlier. His impression was that the present Wittgenstein was more like a creative artist or a religious prophet than a scientist. This Wittgenstein was not interested in formulating and neutralizing objections to conjectures, and was strongly dismissive of the notion of basing philosophy on logic. As Carnap says:

When we found in Wittgenstein's book statements about 'the language,' we interpreted them as referring to an ideal language; and this meant for us a formalized symbolic language. Later Wittgenstein explicitly rejected this view. He had a skeptical and sometimes even a negative view of the importance of a symbolic language for the clarification and correction of the confusions in ordinary language and also in the customary language of philosophers which, as he had shown himself, were often the cause of philosophical puzzles and pseudo-problems.

Carnap and his colleagues in the Circle had read the *Tractatus* as an early expression of Logical Positivism. Their interpretation ignored or at least underemphasized the later parts of the *Tractatus* which are strongly metaphysical, even mystical. As tough-minded, scientifically oriented, and anti-metaphysical thinkers they had marginalized these passages. But for Wittgenstein they were of greater importance than the scientism that the work also unquestionably contains: 'We feel that even if *all possible* scientific questions have been answered, the problems of life have still not been touched at all.' (6.52). He was to state later that the book is all about the mystical and the ethical, i.e., the problems of life, even though, oddly enough, they are only briefly alluded to in the text.

Carnap's account is interesting for another reason. It depicts a profound change that had taken place in Wittgenstein's philosophical orientation. In their interchange, Wittgenstein's comments about science and logic prefigure the kind of outlook he was to develop in *Philosophical Investigations.* Carnap is a careful reporter; he describes Wittgenstein's remarks objectively and accurately, but it is clear that he did not comprehend the creative impulse that motivated them. Given his training and immersion in the *Tractatus,* he cannot be blamed for not recognizing that he was witnessing the birth of a whole new way of thinking. In the *Tractatus* Wittgenstein's view was that colloquial language 'disguises' thought. This is precisely what his later philosophy disavows and it is what he was trying to communicate to Carnap. But it is a central concept in the *Tractatus.* In a wonderful metaphor he depicts everyday language as clothing that hides the body of thought. This is why an ideal symbolic language, like *Principia Mathematica,* must be used instead of everyday discourse if one is to get a solid purchase on the world. As he writes there:

> Colloquial language is part of the human organism and is not less complicated than it.
>
> From it it is humanly impossible to gather immediately the logic of language.
>
> Language disguises the thought; so that from the external form of the clothes one cannot infer the form of the thought that they clothe, because the external form of the clothes is constructed with quite another object than to let the form of the body be recognized.

For the historian this conversation between Carnap and Wittgenstein is fascinating. It indicates that even while Wittgenstein was a school teacher he must have been engaged in thinking about philosophy. The accepted wisdom is that he had completely abandoned interest in the subject after finishing the *Tractatus.* But

Carnap's memoir shows that this interpretation is wrong. It is obvious from their discussion that for some time now Wittgenstein had been exploring a powerful alternative to his previous outlook. Since those new ideas were beginning to percolate in 1927, it is not surprising that in 1929 he decided to return to Cambridge in order to work them out. He was not to abandon the Owl of Minerva again until his death in 1951.

Guilt: homosexuality and being Jewish

In the 1930s, and now living in England, Wittgenstein believed that in face of the increasingly dangerous military developments in Germany and Italy the main hope for humanity lay in the Soviet Union. Like many geniuses his focus on his own work was all-consuming and narrow, and he may well have been politically naive. He seems to have been unaware of, or to have disregarded, the purges that had taken place under Stalin and of that dictator's ruthless authoritarianism. At times he even considered moving to the Soviet Union. With such a prospect in mind, he decided to study Russian and took lessons in Cambridge from a native speaker, Fania Pascal. Mrs. Pascal's 'Wittgenstein: A Personal Memoir,' proffers a different picture of him, less flattering by far, than those we have from Malcolm, Ryle, and von Wright. Her essay begins by describing a confession he made to her in 1937. She writes: 'I can remember two "crimes" to which he confessed: the first had to do with his being Jewish in origin, the second with a wrong he committed when he was a teacher in a village school in Austria ... when he denied that he had done it. On this occasion he did tell a lie, burdening his conscience for ever.' So eleven years after giving false testimony at the Puchberg hearing, Wittgenstein still labored under a sense of guilt.

In recent years, scholars have focused on two areas of his personal behavior about which he suffered profound remorse. As Fania Pascal mentions, one of these concerns his guilt over having concealed the degree to which he was Jewish. The other concerns his homosexuality. The literature on both is extensive. Let us summarize it briefly, beginning with the debate about his homosexuality.

In 1973 the American philosopher W. W. Bartley III published a biography of Wittgenstein that caused a furor. In this work, Bartley had originally set out to discover the degree to which Wittgenstein's activities as a teacher were determined by explicit educational theories. In order to do this, Bartley spent several months in the late 1960s in Vienna and in the rural areas where Wittgenstein had taught. In both places he encountered persons who remembered Wittgenstein, and in the rural areas some persons who had been his pupils forty-five years earlier. Bartley's first-hand interviews with these individuals are the accepted bases of the subsequent scholarship on Wittgenstein's attitudes about teaching. But the book had a related feature that made it a cause célèbre. It contained a description, based on personal interviews with some of these persons, that revealed Wittgenstein not only to have been a homosexual, but promiscuous as well. Bartley also discovered that in Wittgenstein's voluminous notebooks there are passages written in a simple code that mention his sexual encounters and the guilt they occasioned. Bartley attributed Wittgenstein's psychological distress to his inability to control his behavior. Here is a quotation from Bartley's book describing Wittgenstein's sexual proclivities in Vienna in the middle 1920s.

> By walking for ten minutes to the east, down Marxergasse and over the Sophienbrücke (now called the Rotundenbrücke) he could quickly reach the parkland meadows of the Prater, where rough young men were ready to cater to him sexually. Once he had discovered this place, Wittgenstein found to his horror that he could scarcely keep away from it. Several nights each week he would break away from his rooms and make the quick walk to the Prater, possessed, as he put it to friends, by a demon he could barely control. Wittgenstein found he much preferred the sort of rough blunt homosexual youth that he could find strolling in the paths and alleys of the Prater to those ostensibly more refined young men who frequented the Sirk Ecke in the Kartnerstrasse and the neighboring bars at the edge of the inner city. And it was to this particular spot – still used for the same purpose at night, and still about as dangerous – that Wittgenstein was to hie almost as long as he lived in or visited Vienna. Similarly, in later years in England he was from time to time

to flee the fashionable and intellectual young men who were ready to place themselves at his disposal in Cambridge, in favor of the company of tough boys in London pubs (p. 47).

This passage was one of several that caused a ferment, especially since Bartley refused on grounds of confidentiality to name the sources of his information. Supporters of Wittgenstein were outraged. They provided testimony from psychiatrists that Wittgenstein was not a homosexual. They even engaged in personal attacks on Bartley. Defenders of Bartley took a different position. They suggested that Wittgenstein's literary executors had engaged in a cover-up by blacking out or by not releasing passages in his note-books about his sexual life. In support of this thesis, they quoted a remark by Professor Elizabeth Anscombe, one of the three execu-tors, in a letter she wrote to the architect Paul Englemann: 'If by pressing a button it could have been secured that people would not concern themselves with his personal life I should have pressed the button.' Why there might have been such a cover-up is almost impossible to explain because Wittgenstein's behavior before and after his return in 1929, was the subject of gossip long before Bartley's book was published. In her 1937 memoir Fania Pascal mentions that she and her husband wondered whether Wittgenstein was a homosexual. In their view, and as far as she knew in the view of 'all others who knew him,' he was not. To them, consumed by his work, he appeared 'a person of unforced chastity':

He became the freest of men, certainly with full freedom of choice where to live, and with whom to consort. Yet he had to do his work unremittingly, and for this he depended on a small select band of pupils and disciples: this was the only tie that bound him and this he accepted. If it should be asked, was that tie in any form of manner a homosexual one (a question much in fashion nowadays), I can only say that to my husband and myself, and as far as I know to all others who knew him, Wittgenstein always appeared a person of *unforced* chastity. There was in fact something of *noli me tangere* about him, so that one cannot imagine anyone who would ever dare as much as to pat him on the back, nor can one imagine him in need of the normal physical expressions of affection. In him everything was sublimated to an extraordinary degree.

Their view differs from Ray Monk's. Monk has written the most extensive and detailed biography of Wittgenstein. It is entitled: *Ludwig Wittgenstein: The Duty of Genius* (1990). In its last chapter there is a sensitive, informed discussion of the homosexuality issue. Monk provides overwhelming evidence that Wittgenstein was a homosexual and names some of the individuals who were his lovers 'over a period of thirty years or so' (e.g., David Pinsent, Francis Skinner, and Ben Richards). However, Monk is sceptical about Bartley's contention that Wittgenstein was promiscuous. He does not deny that he was. Instead, his view is that since Bartley refused to name his informants one must suspend judgment about his claims. For Monk, then, the issue about Wittgenstein's homosexuality is settled, but that about his alleged promiscuity remains open. Most scholars who are not actively engaged in the debate put a different spin on it. They hold almost unanimously that the question of Wittgenstein's sexual orientation has little relevance for understanding his philosophy. In the major texts, the *Tractatus*, *Philosophical Investigations, Remarks on the Foundations of Mathematics, Zettel*, and *On Certainty*, there is no talk about homosexuality or indeed about sexuality at all. The issues with which he was obsessed are entirely of a different order.

Let us look now at his guilt about being Jewish. This is a more complicated matter. It has two parts. First, Wittgenstein was fully aware that he was three-quarters Jewish. He told Mrs. Pascal that most people who knew him, including many of his friends, took him to be three-quarters Aryan and one-quarter Jewish, and that he had done nothing to correct this misapprehension. His guilt seems to have arisen in part because of the anti-Semitism that was sweeping Austria and Germany in the 1920s and 1930s, and his feeling that he should have been forthright about his background. The question of his heritage was uncovered by Bartley and later confirmed by other investigators. Wittgenstein was baptized a Catholic at birth and died as a Catholic. But early in the nineteenth century the family converted from Judaism to Catholicism, and all of its members were aware of this history. Here are the facts as adduced by Bartley:

Another family tree, however, prepared in Jerusalem since the war, reports that Hermann Christian Wittgenstein was the son of Moses Meier Wittgenstein, Jew of Korbach, and the grandson of Moses Meier, Jew of Laasphe and Korbach. Although the records of the Jewish community in Korbach were destroyed when the SS burned the Korback synagogue in November 1938, family tradition, comments in the dairy of Hermine Wittgenstein, and significant facts – such as that the Wittgenstein family in Vienna possesses portraits of Moses Meier and his wife Brendel Simon – suggest that this line of descent is correct. If so, Ludwig Wittgenstein was indeed three-quarters Jewish, the family name having been changed from Meier to Wittgenstein in 1808 when Napoleonic decrees required that Jews adopt a surname.

I will say no more about this matter. The second part of what might be called 'the Jewish problem' does not concern Wittgenstein's feelings of guilt, because the issue arose after his death. In the early 1990s some scholars charged that in one of his books, *Culture and Value*, Wittgenstein made vicious anti-Semitic remarks. Ray Monk, for example, says: 'Were they not written by Wittgenstein, many of his pronouncements on the nature of Jews would be understood as nothing more than the rantings of a fascist anti-Semite.' Gerhard D. Wasserman makes similar allegations. He states that 'Wittgenstein absorbed like a sponge, and re-emitted, anti-Semitic lies, past and present,' and that 'he accepted uncritically, and propounded dogmatically, as if true, anti-Semitic views that were already widely current in Germany and Austria in the 1920's.'

In a paper, 'Was Wittgenstein an Anti-Semite?' (1999), Bela Szabados examines these charges and the textual evidence for them. He contends that they are groundless, and indeed are exaggerations based on a misreading of remarks that Wittgenstein made in *Culture and Value*. I myself have looked into the matter and agree with Szabados. The main evidence that both Monk and Wasserman cite consists of twelve brief passages that appear in *Culture and Value*. Most of these are commendatory about Jews (e.g., 'The Jew is a desert region, but underneath its thin layer of rock lies the molten lava of spirit and intellect.') In another passage, which is mildly negative, Wittgenstein openly acknowledges that he is a Jew ('Even the greatest of Jewish thinkers is no more than talented, Myself for instance.') I do not find anything in *Culture and Value* corresponding to the 'rantings of a fascist anti-Semite.' I conclude, concurring with Szabados, that the charges carry very little weight.

Wittgenstein was not a raving anti-Semite. Of course, it does not follow from this fact that he did not have anti-Jewish prejudices of a lesser order. It is well known that some Jews have a disparaging attitude toward other Jews, and it is possible that Wittgenstein fell into this category. This is precisely the thesis that David Stern has argued in a brilliant paper, 'The Significance of Jewishness for Wittgenstein's Philosophy' (2000). Stern's paper is the most probing analysis of what the notion of being a Jew meant to Wittgenstein, and how he reacted to the knowledge that in some important sense he was three-quarters Jewish. Stern ends his essay with the following paragraphs:

> Antisemitism is strikingly akin to a Wittgensteinian philosophical problem: it arises from taken-for-granted prejudices and the misuse of language, and can only be dissolved by changing people's lives. The philosophical significance of Jewishness for Wittgenstein is not primarily that he thought of his philosophy as Jewish, but that Jewishness was not a problem that he was able to write about philosophically.
>
> Finally, we can briefly return to the question: Was Wittgenstein a Jew? My Hertzian answer is that we would be better off distinguishing different senses of the term, and reflecting on their role in his life and in our own. Wittgenstein's problematic Jewishness is as much a product of our problematic concerns as his. There is no doubt that Wittgenstein was of Jewish descent; it is equally clear that he was not a practicing Jew. But insofar as he thought of himself as Jewish, he did so in terms of the antisemitic prejudices of this time. It would have been good if he could have untangled those prejudices, but he did not do so.

The final days, 1929–1951

In 1929 Wittgenstein decided to enroll as a Ph.D. student at Cambridge. He submitted the *Tractatus*, which had been published seven years earlier, as his doctoral dissertation. Moore and Russell agreed to serve as the examiners on his committee. According to Hermine's account the exam seems to have been something of a farce. It 'consisted of the professors asking Ludwig to explain to them passages from his book.' At its conclusion, Moore wrote: 'It is my personal opinion that Mr. Wittgenstein's thesis is a work of genius; but, be that as it may, it is certainly well up to the standard required for the Cambridge degree of "Doctor of Philosophy".' So Wittgenstein passed and shortly afterward was hired as a lecturer in philosophy.

His first lecture was given on 20 January 1930, and the course was called – as all of his subsequently were – 'philosophy.' Wittgenstein's way of 'lecturing' was so unusual that the word is probably a misdescription. He talked without notes in a kind of self-absorbed monologue that his auditors felt privileged to overhear. The presentations were not held in a formal classroom but in his sitting room in Trinity College. In the middle of a sentence he would stop, saying, 'just a minute let me think,' and would sit down for a few minutes, struggling with an idea he was trying to express. Occasionally he would accuse himself of stupidity. There were long silences as he battled to formulate a sentence, with the group sitting silently and spell-bound awaiting for the contest to issue in something they could chew on. About fifteen students and the occasional colleague made up his audience. The most famous don to attend was G. E. Moore, who was given the only armchair in the room (everyone else sat in deckchairs). Moore was a faithful participant, coming to each lecture for three years. He took extensive notes that were later published as *Wittgenstein's Lectures, 1930–33*. These are important documents since they provide the clearest picture of Wittgenstein's new methodology, and I shall discuss them in Chapter 3.

Wittgenstein's intensity, and the effort to express his ideas, made an indelible impression on all who listened to him. His pattern of speech, a kind of stammering he was given to, and his labored facial expressions, were imitated by students and dons alike. Most were awed by the intellectual struggle they were witnessing. But some felt otherwise. Gilbert Ryle mentions that veneration for Wittgenstein was so uncontrolled that Ryle's references to any other philosopher were greeted with jeers. In his autobiography he says: 'This contempt for thoughts other than Wittgenstein's seemed to me pedagogically disastrous for the students and unhealthy for Wittgenstein himself. It made me resolve, not indeed to be a philosophical polyglot, but to avoid being a monoglot; and most of all to avoid being one's monoglot's echo, even though he was a genius and a friend.' In his autobiography, C. D. Broad implied that Wittgenstein was something of a poseur who deliberately played to the audience, and relished the attention he received in return. Broad wrote: 'The one duty which I willingly neglected was to attend the weekly meetings of the Moral Sciences Club ... I was not prepared to spend hours every week in a thick atmosphere of cigarette-smoke, while Wittgenstein punctually went through his hoops, and the faithful as punctually "wondered with a foolish face of praise".' But like Ryle, Broad – a tough-minded professional if there ever was one – recognized that Wittgenstein was a genius. When the issue of whether Wittgenstein should be appointed to replace Moore arose, he said: 'To refuse the chair to Wittgenstein would be like refusing Einstein a chair of physics.'

Throughout the 1930s Wittgenstein's reputation spread like a wave, whose center was Cambridge but whose edges extended first to Oxford and then beyond. All this without any publications except the *Tractatus* of 1922 and his short paper on logical form of 1929. At first it was the brilliance of the remarks he made in conferences and seminars that impressed people. Over time Wittgenstein came to dominate these sessions. Philosophers came from all over the UK to hear him talk. It was as if Socrates had suddenly shown up in England. Like Socrates, Wittgenstein's powerful personality and philosophical originality attracted a coterie of followers and admirers. But there was another factor that greatly spread his fame: two sets of lecture notes that a small group of his students had taken. These were typescripts enclosed in paper covers that were, respectively, blue and brown. They were later published and are known as the *Blue Book* and the *Brown Book*. Many copies were made of these notes and by the late 1930s they were in wide circulation. When I was a graduate student, I was told by some veteran faculty members that they were common currency in Berkeley before the Second

World War. The two sets of notes differ considerably but they share a common feature: both are applications of the new method that was to receive its canonical expression in *Philosophical Investigations* published posthumously in 1953.

Moore and Wittgenstein had close relations after Wittgenstein's return to Cambridge in 1929. Though Moore said that Russell influenced him more than any other philosopher, he was enormously impressed by Wittgenstein. In his autobiography, Moore said of Wittgenstein: 'When I did get to know him, I soon came to feel that he was much cleverer at philosophy than I was and not only cleverer, but also much more profound, and with a much better insight into the sort of inquiry which was really important and best worth pursuing, and into the best method of pursuing such inquiries …' When Moore retired in 1939, Wittgenstein replaced him as professor. Before he could begin teaching, war broke out. As he had done in 1914, Wittgenstein immediately left academia and volunteered his assistance, but this time, of course, to the English. Now fifty, he was too old to be a soldier, but he still insisted on contributing in any capacity that he could. He served for a time as a porter at Guy's Hospital in London and then as a laboratory assistant in Newcastle. In 1944, as the war was winding down, he returned to Cambridge. But he was never happy as a professor and resigned his chair in 1947 in order to pursue his research. That Wittgenstein was already a legend in his time is confirmed by his having been granted such a prestigious position without any publications other than the two I mentioned above.

After he resigned his professorship, his health began to deteriorate. He not only suffered attacks of painful indigestion but severe mental stress. In his letters we read such comments as:

> Feel unwell. Am frightened of the onset of insanity … My nerves, I'm afraid often misbehave. Of course they're tired and old nerves. My work, on the whole, goes fairly well. Again it's the work of an old man; for, though I am not really old, I have, somehow an old soul. May it be granted to me that my body doesn't survive my soul.

Despite these complaints he felt well enough in 1949 to visit Norman Malcolm who was then teaching at Cornell. This, as we shall see in Chapter 4, turned out to be a significant journey. It stimulated Wittgenstein to write *On Certainty*, his last and one of his greatest books. He worked on it for another year and a half and inserted the last seven entries in it just two days before he died. In November 1949, having returned to England from the United States, he was diagnosed with cancer of the prostate. The original diagnosis was optimistic. It was thought that with modern hormone therapy he could live in reasonably good health for another five or six years. But, as sometimes happens with this disease, he deteriorated rapidly and died on 29 April 1951. His sixty-second birthday had fallen on the previous day. Before going into a coma he said to those attending him: 'Tell them I've had a wonderful life.'

chapter Two

The *Tractatus*

Introduction

I turn now to Wittgenstein's first great idea, a notion that appears in the *Tractatus Logico-Philosophicus* of 1922. Put in its simplest form that idea consists of a theory that lays down the conditions for significant utterance about the world. One of Wittgenstein's eminent predecessors, the German philosopher Immanuel Kant (1724–1804), had developed a similar but nonetheless fundamentally different view. Kant was an epistemologist. His concern was to formulate the conditions that explained how *knowledge* of the world is possible. But in the *Tractatus* Wittgenstein is interested in ontology, i.e., in what the world is fundamentally like and how *meaningful discourse* about it is possible. As Wittgenstein realized, any inquiry into how we can acquire knowledge presupposes that knowledge claims are cognitively significant. There is thus, from a logical point of view, a prior requirement that must be satisfied before Kant's investigations can be regarded as complete. One must state what it is for any proposition to be cognitively significant. No philosopher before Wittgenstein had recognized that this is so and in the *Tractatus* he committed himself to meeting this challenge. The resulting theory is his great idea, namely to describe the conditions that must be satisfied before significant utterance about the world is possible. Kant called his account of such conditions a 'transcendental argument.' One can say, paralleling Kant's terminology, that Wittgenstein is proferring a transcendental argument about significance.

But in order to explain what Wittgenstein's theory is and why it is important I will retrace, though in more detail, some steps I took in the previous chapter. In effect, I will have to return to the development of mathematical logic by Frege and Russell around the turn of the century. This is necessary because Wittgenstein's great idea is based upon the insights he derived from his study of their logical systems before he began to write the *Tractatus*. His theory can thus only be understood in the light of the exciting developments in logic that had taken place, and were taking place, when he became Russell's student in Cambridge in 1911.

The question Wittgenstein's great idea is designed to answer is inherited, as we shall see below, from Frege and Russell: '*How is it possible that by uttering a series of noises or writing down a series of marks on paper one can refer to objects in the world and communicate to others what one is referring to?*' The traditional answer to the question is that there is a direct correspondence between the words that occur in sentences and the objects in the world that one is speaking about. Thus, according to that conception, when one uses the word 'Plato' in a sentence such as 'Plato was the author of *The Republic*,' one is referring to a particular Greek philosopher. The sentence is also obviously meaningful. It is meaningful because such words as 'Plato,' and 'The Republic,' etc., *mean* the actual things being spoken about and the sentence is a composite of their meanings. One is thus applying the word 'Plato' to a particular person, and the words 'The Republic' to a book that Plato wrote and such applications amount to saying that the words mean their corresponding objects. According to this intuitively plausible account significant utterance about the world is possible because there is a one-to-one correspondence or isomorphism between the linguistic units in an utterance and the objects those linguistic expressions refer to or pick out.

Unfortunately, plausible though it is, this intuitive account of the relationship between language and reality breaks down when confronted with a simple counter-example. The counter-example is one that the ancient Greeks were already aware of and it gives rise to a much deeper problem about the relationship between language and reality. In Plato's *Sophist* the counter-example is posed as follows: 'How is it possible to speak meaningfully and even truly about non-being?' Now why should this question show that the intuitive account will not do? The answer is that it assumes that a person can refer to something only if that something exists. But by definition non-being is nothing at all. In such a case reference is impossible, and if so, one's words will lack meaning. Failing to mean they cannot be true of anything either. But in everyday discourse human beings do speak meaningfully and truly about the non-existent. Such sentences as 'Santa Claus does not exist,' and 'Hamlet was a prince of Denmark,' are examples of such uses. Yet if 'Santa Claus' and 'Hamlet' fail to refer, how are meaning and truth possible? This is the deeper problem and it shows that the simple and intuitive theory about the relationship between language and world is unacceptable. Accordingly, an alternative theory must be developed to accommodate the actual facts of everyday language usage. This is the problem Wittgenstein set out to solve.

The Frege/Russell solutions

Though the challenge about non-being continued to bedevil philosophy, compelling solutions were possible only with the development of the new logic that I described in the previous chapter. First Frege in a paper entitled 'On Sense and Reference,' ('Über Sinn und Bedeutung') published in 1892, and then Russell in a series of papers and books, such as 'On Denoting' (1905) and *Principia Mathematica* (1910–1913) offered solutions to the problem. The two approaches differ in essentials but both turn on the analysis of linguistic phrases containing the word 'the' in the singular, such as 'the pen I am now holding,' or 'the game I saw yesterday.' Such phrases connote uniqueness; that is, they refer to exactly one pen or exactly one game, and so forth. Following Russell's usage let us call such phrases 'definite descriptions,' or even more simply 'descriptions.' The Frege/Russell solutions are thus two different versions of the theory of descriptions. We shall describe both in what follows, beginning with Frege's.

Their influence on Wittgenstein's great idea is palpable and in the following sections we shall describe that relationship.

Frege solved the problem of non-being by drawing a tripartite distinction between: (1) linguistic expressions, (2) what they mean, and (3) what they refer to. In effect, he was making the point that the concept of 'meaning' is ambiguous: sometimes in speaking about the meaning of a linguistic unit one is speaking about its connotation or sense (i.e., the idea it expresses), and sometimes about its referent (i.e., the object or thing it is referring to or mentioning). Accordingly, he invented a technical vocabulary to discriminate between these two uses of 'meaning.' The connotative use he called 'Sinn' and the referential use 'Bedeutung.' In ordinary German they are often used as synonyms for 'meaning.' But they are sharply different in Frege's technical employment. The difference can be brought out as follows. The term 'the greatest natural number' has a certain meaning, or connotation, or Sinn. We can grasp the idea or sense it expresses and even translate it into a different language. In Italian, for example, it would be translated as 'il piu grande numero naturale.' But there is no greatest such number, so there is no object that the phrase refers to. In such a case, Frege says that the phrase has no referent or Bedeutung. In contrast, the phrase 'the morning star' has both a Sinn and a Bedeutung. The sense it expresses is that of an astral body that appears in the morning sky. Its Bedeutung is the planet Venus.

Scholars have translated Frege's distinction between Sinn and Bedeutung into English in various ways. Sinn has been rendered as 'sense,' 'meaning,' 'concept,' 'intention,' 'connotation,' and 'designation.' Bedeutung appears in the literature as 'meaning,' 'referent,' 'nominatum,' 'object,' 'extension,' and 'denotation.' In what follows we shall use 'sense' and 'referent' as corresponding to the German expressions Sinn and Bedeutung, respectively.

Frege's basic idea is that every well-formed linguistic expression has a Sinn, and many also have a Bedeutung. But the important point, as the example of 'the greatest natural number' illustrates, is that some may not have a Bedeutung.

With this distinction in hand we can see how he deals with the problem of non-being. In referring to Hamlet, for instance, we can render the sense of the name as a descriptive phrase. Its sense would be something like 'the main male character in the play *Hamlet* by Shakespeare.' The sentence 'Hamlet is Prince of Denmark' is perfectly significant, since it expresses a sense. But Frege asserts that such a sentence is neither true nor false, because 'Hamlet' lacks a Bedeutung. His account thus explains how a linguistic unit can be meaningful even when it lacks a referent. The distinction applies not only to proper names but to larger units of language as well, such as descriptions and sentences. Each of these can be said to have a Sinn and, depending on the state of the world, a referent or Bedeutung. In the case of a declarative sentence, its normal sense (Sinn) is a proposition, and its referent (Bedeutung) is either the True or the False, depending on whether it is true or false. Descriptive phrases express a sense and have a referent if something exists that they pick out. All individual words or grammatically correct combinations of words he called 'names.' Thus, a declarative sentence is a name on his account, and if true, names the True, and if false, names the False.

Frege regarded the fact that some names in natural languages lack referents as a defect, and as one important reason why philosophy should be done in an ideal language. In the ideal language of mathematical logic the defect is repaired. Each term has both a Sinn and a Bedeutung, even if in some cases, as with respect to 'the greatest natural number,' the Bedeutung is an artificial 'entity,' such as Aleph Null or A*.

Russell, differing from Frege, denied that genuine proper names, like 'Venus,' possessed connotative meaning or Sinn. According to him they mean the object they name (i.e., denote or refer to). The bearer of a proper name is thus the meaning of the name on this account. In Fregean terminology, Russell is denying that a proper name has a Sinn and is asserting instead that it only has a Bedeutung. His solution to the problem of non-being, given this usage, was unexpected, ingenious, and complex to explain. The theory claims that putative names, such as 'Hamlet' or 'Odysseus,' are not real names but descriptive phrases and therefore sentences containing genuine proper names must be analysed differently from those containing descriptions. According to Russell, traditional philosophers failed to distinguish descriptive phrases from genuine names because both seem to have the same functions. Both can be used to mention or pick out or refer to the same object. Thus in the sentences 'Clinton is tall,' and 'The American president in the year 2000 is tall,' both the name and the description pick out Bill Clinton.

Though definite descriptions and proper names may sometimes denote the same individual or place, Russell argued that their logical functions are entirely disparate. Thus, a speaker who in the year 2000 asserted 'the President of the United States is tall,' would have used the definite description 'the President of the United States' to refer to Bill Clinton. But that phrase is not Clinton's name; it could be used on different occasions to refer to different individuals. If Bill Clinton had been replaced as President in 2000 by another tall person, that phrase would then have picked out someone other than Clinton. Indeed, descriptive phrases can be used without picking out anything. 'The greatest natural number' does not pick out anything, since there is a strict proof that no such number exists. 'The present King of France' if intended to refer to a twentieth-century monarch would also lack a referent.

Russell's career as a philosopher stretched over seven decades, and in nearly all of these he produced modifications of the theory of descriptions. Nevertheless he always drew a sharp distinction between proper names and descriptions. In some of his middle period writings – as in 'Knowledge by Description and Knowledge by Acquaintance' (1914), and in *The Philosophy of Logical Atomism* (1918) – the theory took an epistemological turn. In this period Russell held that a proper name is something that applies only to an object with which one is directly acquainted. He said that such demonstrative pronouns as 'this,' and 'that,' uttered on particular occasions, are what he called 'logically' proper names, whereas a 'grammatically' proper name, such as 'Julius Caesar,' is not a logically proper name since nobody alive today is or could be directly acquainted with Caesar. Everything we know about Caesar we know via descriptions found in books, such as Livy's *History of Rome*. Therefore, 'Julius Caesar' is a covert or abbreviated description, not a real name. This continued to be Russell's view until his death in 1970.

Despite these changes, Russell, throughout his career, never deviated from the position that the so-called 'names' of fictive characters are not real names but are abbreviated descriptions. 'Odysseus,' 'Hamlet,' 'Santa Claus,' etc. fall into this category. They are not the names of persons, but appear in history, mythology, or literature, via legends, stories or literary accounts. In the play *Hamlet*, by Shakespeare, the author proffers a description of a certain character. In that drama, the apparent name 'Hamlet' is thus an abbreviation for a description in the words provided by the playwright. Russell also consistently held that no matter how the distinction between proper names and descriptions is drawn it can be demonstrated that sentences containing proper names and sentences containing descriptions mean different things. And this can be shown by translating the respective sentences into an ideal language, such as that of *Principia*, where the difference is perspicuous and takes a purely symbolic form.

Thus, 'Bill Clinton is tall' is of the logical form 'Fa.' This is a singular sentence, containing a logical constant 'a' which stands for a proper name, and a predicate term 'F' that stands for a property. When the constant and the predicate are given descriptive meaning, as in the sentence 'Clinton is tall,' we see that both sentences are ascribing a certain property to a particular individual. Both are thus logically singular sentences. They can be contrasted with 'The present King of France is tall,' which is grammatically a singular sentence but which, when translated into logical notation, is not of the form 'Fa.' It has a completely different form. In English it means the same as 'At least one person and at most one person is now male and monarch of France, and whoever is male and monarch of France is tall.' It is thus not logically a singular sentence but a complex general one. In symbolic notation it would be expressed as a conjunction of three sentences, one of them asserting the existence of a French monarch.

(i) $((\exists x)(MFx))$ (At least one thing is now male, monarch of France.)

(ii) $((((x)(y))\ ((MFx \wedge MFy \supset (x=y))))$ (At most one thing is now male, monarch of France.)

(iii) $(((x))\ ((MFx \supset (Tx)))$ (Whoever is now male, monarch of France is tall.)

In the English sentence 'The present King of France is tall,' the word 'the' expresses singularity, referring to one object as monarch of France. Singularity (the concept of 'the') is captured by sentences (i) and (ii). To say that one and only one object is present King of France is to say that at least one such object now exists and also that not more than one does. If there is such an object then (i) and (ii) are true; and if the object has the property ascribed to it then the whole sentence, 'The present King of France is tall,' is true. The whole sentence is false under any one of three conditions: If there is no such object then (i) is false; if there is more than one such object (ii) is false; and, finally, if there is exactly one such object but it does not possess the property of being tall then (iii) is false. But in logic if any conjunct of a compound sentence is false, the whole sentence is false. So in this case because the King of France does not exist, 'The present King of France is tall' is false. But if false it is nevertheless meaningful. It is meaningful because each of the three sentences that unpack its meaning is meaningful. This analysis is Russell's solution to the problem of non-being. It demonstrates how a sentence can be significant even when one of its key terms lacks a referent.

Apart from arguing that names and descriptions are to be analyzed differently, Russell throughout his long career proposed a host of arguments to demonstrate this point. As he writes in *Introduction to Mathematical Philosophy* (1918):

> A proposition containing a description is not identical with what that proposition becomes when a name is substituted, even if the name names the same object as the description describes. 'Scott is the author of *Waverley*' is obviously a different proposition from 'Scott is Scott': the first is a fact in literary history, the second a trivial truism. And if we put anyone other than Scott in place of 'the author of *Waverley*' our proposition would become false, and would therefore certainly no longer be the same proposition. (p. 174)

The point of the argument is to show that 'Scott is Scott' and 'Scott is the author of *Waverley*' are different propositions, and that this is so because the proper name 'Scott' and the description 'the author of *Waverley*' play logically different roles. Russell's argument has found widespread acceptance among philosophers of language, and until recently it was regarded as sound. But in my judgment it is not. Consider the following counter-example, for instance.

(i)   'The author of *Waverley* is the author of *Waverley*.'
(ii) 'The author of *Waverley* is the author of *Ivanhoe*' is a fact in literary history.
(iii) If we put anyone other than the author of *Waverley* in place of 'the author of *Ivanhoe*' then (ii) would become false.

This argument is a mirror image of Russell's. One can see immediately that 'The author of *Waverley* is the author of *Waverley*' and 'The author of *Waverley* is the author of *Ivanhoe*' differ in meaning in that the first is trivial and the second is not. The latter proposition is not trivial since one might not know that the author of *Waverley* also authored a book called *Ivanhoe*. Yet, in contrast, it is a trivial truth that the author of *Waverley* is the author of *Waverley*. One can also agree with Russell that in general there is a difference between proper names and descriptions. 'The first-born child of John Smith' may refer to Robin Smith, but that locution is not her name.

If my counter-argument is correct, Russell's analysis of why the two propositions differ in meaning is flawed. The difference clearly does not turn on the difference between names and descriptions since the counter-argument arrives at exactly his distinctions and yet uses only descriptions. There is thus something wrong with Russell's line of reasoning. Nonetheless, even if Russell's argument does not succeed, there are other reasons for thinking that his version of the theory of descriptions is unquestionably a major achievement. Among these reasons are the following four:

First, it shows that an ideal language can not only articulate the ordinary sentences of natural languages but also that it can reveal distinctions that such languages conceal.

Second, this fact implies that one must distinguish surface grammar from a deeper logical grammar that expresses the real meaning of such sentences. According to this deeper grammar, definite descriptions are not names, and sentences containing definitive descriptions are not singular but general sentences. This finding has direct philosophical import. It clears up a second puzzle about existence, namely, how it is possible, with consistency, to deny the existence of something. Suppose an atheist says: 'God does not exist.' It would seem that the atheist is presupposing by his very words that there exists something, a God, that does not exist; so he seems to be contradicting himself. Russell showed that in this sentence 'God' is not a name but an abbreviated description for (on a Judeo-Christian conception) 'the x that is all powerful, all wise, and benevolent.' The atheist's sentence can now be read as saying: 'There is nothing that is all powerful, all wise, and benevolent.' The apparent name, 'God,' has disappeared from the atheist's sentence. The analysis thus allows a philosophical position to be expressed without falling into inconsistency. This result has similar implications for skepticism. It allows a radical skeptic to deny that knowledge is attainable without presupposing that there is such a thing as knowledge.

Third, if one looks at the preceding analysis of the sentence 'The present King of France is tall,' one will see that the phrase 'The present King of France' no longer appears as a single unit in any of the three sentences that taken together give its meaning. This means that the phrase 'The present King of France' has been eliminated and replaced by a complex of quantifiers, variables, and predicates. If it were a proper name it would not be eliminable. Because they are eliminable definite descriptions were called 'incomplete symbols' by Russell. His theory of descriptions is thus a theory about the nature and function of incomplete symbols.

Fourth, it will be noted that each of the analyzing sentences is a general sentence and each is meaningful. This fact is key to understanding how a sentence whose subject term lacks a referent can be meaningful.

In the light of the preceding account, one can summarize Russell's solution to the problem of non-being. Once one sees that 'the present King of France' is a description then there need be nothing that the phrase refers to; and therefore from the fact that a sentence containing the phrase is meaningful, it does not follow that its grammatical subject term denotes anything. There is thus no need to worry about the status of such 'entities' as The Present King of France, Hamlet, Medusa, and Santa Claus. By means of this analysis the problem of non-being has been disposed of.

The influence of Frege and Russell on Wittgenstein

When Wittgenstein began to study logic he was much impressed by its capacity to solve difficult problems, and especially by the ingenuity that both Frege and Russell had shown in their differing versions of the theory of descriptions. In the brief Preface to the *Tractatus* he expresses his admiration for them, writing: 'I will only mention that to the great works of Frege and the writings of my friend Bertrand Russell I owe in large measure the stimulation of my thoughts.'

He accepted from both of them the notion that an ideal language, such as *Principia Mathematica*, was needed for the resolution of philosophical problems, and that one must distinguish the surface grammar of language from a deeper logical grammar that expresses the real meanings of linguistic expressions. But he went beyond these insights in uncovering further powers of mathematical logic. He generalized their results into a synoptic philosophical theory about the relationship between language and reality based on logic. Though he does not give a name to this theory I will call it his Logical Atomism. I do so because, as I mentioned in the previous chapter, Russell was later to call the doctrine by that name and in so doing attributed its genesis to Wittgenstein. It is clear that many of the ideas that Russell advances in *The Philosophy of Logical Atomism* of 1918 are in the *Tractatus* and were probably developed by Wittgenstein as early as 1913 in the year he spent in Norway.

Once he had arrived at this general theory about how language connects to reality, Wittgenstein realized that it could be used to define the limits of what could significantly be said about the world. Let us trace that story.

Wittgenstein's Logical Atomism and the picture theory

Wittgenstein does not use the phrase 'Logical Atomism' to describe this view. It is a term that Russell coined. But Wittgenstein does frequently refer to what he calls *atomic facts* in the *Tractatus* and many commentators believe that Russell inherited the name from Wittgenstein's pre-*Tractatus* notebooks. It is also important to stress that in using such terms as 'atomism,' or 'atomic,' or their variants, neither Wittgenstein nor Russell was speaking about 'atoms' in the usual scientific sense of that locution.

Instead, they used these expressions in two different ways. First, both opposed the forms of idealism that dominated British philosophy at the beginning of the twentieth century. The major idealists, such as F. H. Bradley (1846–1924) and J. E. McTaggart (1866–1925) were monists. They held that reality constitutes a totality whose parts are internally and necessarily related to one another and cannot be separated without distortion, even for descriptive purposes. One implication of this doctrine is that there are no independent, discrete facts, and therefore that no single statement about any particular feature of the world is either wholly true or wholly false. Insofar as the notions of truth or falsity can be applied to individual propositions any one of them is at most partially true or partially false. The only wholly true proposition that can be uttered is about the absolute, i.e., the totality of what exists.

Their monism is the view that there is one and only one reality and that is the absolute. Their idealism is the view that reality is mental so that nothing exists independently of being conceived or perceived. The earliest arguments against this position were developed by G. E. Moore who argued that there are mind-independent, discrete facts composed of particular things. Both Wittgenstein and Russell concurred with Moore. Such atomic facts are composed of elements that Wittgenstein calls 'objects.' As he says in entry 2.01 of the *Tractatus*, 'An atomic fact is a combination of objects (entities, things).' These facts are thus the 'atoms' that make up the world. Wittgenstein's version of this position first occurs in 1.1. He says: 'The world is the totality of facts, not of things.' Such facts can be individuated and described, and it is therefore possible to make wholly true or wholly false statements about them. In holding, like Moore, that it is possible to isolate certain facts from a supposedly unitary background, Wittgenstein and Russell were using the terms 'atomic' and 'atomism' in contrast to the holistic views of their idealistic opponents.

They also used these terms in a second sense. I will say more about it below in connection with their commitments to an 'ideal language.' Suffice it to say for the moment that both thought that colloquial language, e.g., English, French or Italian, is defective for grappling with philosophical problems. But mathematical logic for them was a specially constructed language that lacks these defects and its use is necessary for seeing 'the world rightly,' as Wittgenstein was graphically to say at the end of the *Tractatus*. Such a formal language constructs complex propositions from simple ones by means of the logical connectives, 'and', 'or', 'if … then,' and so forth. In principle, the meaning of every complex statement can thus be reduced to the meaning of its simple components. The simple propositions can thus be thought of as atoms and the complex ones as molecules that are composed of them. Wittgenstein calls the former 'elementary propositions.' When true, they denote atomic facts. Furthermore, the truth or falsity of a complex proposition is a direct function of the truth or falsity of its elementary constituents. As Wittgenstein puts it in 4.52, 'So, in some sense, one could say, that all propositions are generalizations of the elementary propositions.' Wittgenstein's idea is technically called a 'recursive theory,' i.e., a system which allows the reduction of complex linguistic structures to a limited set of basic units.

Wittgenstein took a further step. He argued that if we analyse the structure of an elementary proposition, we will find it is composed of objects that 'hang together' like the links in a chain. In such a formal language, a proper name directly denotes an object, and the name means the object. As he says:

> In propositions thoughts can be so expressed that to the objects of the thoughts correspond the elements of the propositional sign. These elements I call 'simple signs' and the proposition 'completely analyzed.' The simple signs employed in propositions are called names. The name means the object. The object is its meaning. To the configuration of the simple signs in the propositional sign corresponds the configuration of the objects in the state of affairs. In the proposition the name represents the object. (3.2–3.22)

This passage describes one of the two main ways that language 'hooks up' to reality. The first link is by means of proper names. They have meaning (Bedeutung) and directly pick out particular objects in the world. Here he is following Russell's treatment of proper names. The other major link is the elementary proposition. It has sense (Sinn). Here he is following Frege. But Wittgenstein now adds something new. An elementary proposition directly refers to or picks out *atomic facts*. Accordingly, the second use of 'atomic' by Wittgenstein refers to the facts denoted by elementary propositions. His Logical Atomism thus sharply distinguishes between the real world and the language that can be used to refer to it. Russell was later to concur. Unlike the monists, both Russell and Wittgenstein drew a sharp contrast between an independently existing reality and the human capacity by means of language to speak about it.

There is, however, one important respect in which the Wittgensteinian and Russellian forms of Logical Atomism differ. This concerns Wittgenstein's explanation of how elementary propositions actually pick out or refer to atomic facts. Scholars call the account 'the picture theory.' No such theory is found in Russell. Wittgenstein's view is that elementary propositions – as distinct from propositions in ordinary language – are *pictures* of atomic facts. Since on his view the totality of existent atomic facts is the world (2.04), and since the totality of true elementary propositions describes all the atomic facts there are, the totality of elementary propositions is a 'model of reality' (2.12). As he says: 'Thus the picture is linked with reality; it reaches up to it.' What Wittgenstein is stressing is that the fundamental connection between language and reality is via a picturing relationship. This theory of the picturing relationship between language and reality provides a further reason why it is necessary to use a formal language for philosophical purposes. It is only in a symbolic language, such as *Principia Mathematica*, that one can formulate elementary propositions and therefore it is only by means of such a language that one can attain an accurate picture of the world.

How did Wittgenstein arrive at the picture theory? According to some of his biographers the idea occurred to him while he was serving on the Eastern Front in the First World War. According to the story, he read a report in a magazine concerning an automobile accident in Paris in which an architectural model of the accident was presented before a judge. Wittgenstein was struck by the fact that the model was able to represent the accident because of the correspondence between its components and the persons, automobiles, and places actually involved in the incident. He thus suddenly realized that a proposition could serve a similar function. It could provide a picture of the world through a correlation of its linguistic elements with the actual persons and things it speaks about. Using this analogy, he decided that a proposition could be thought of as a picture of reality. Hence, the picture theory was born.

Wittgenstein's account of the picturing relationship occupies a substantial portion of the early parts of the *Tractatus*. Starting at 2.1 with the remark 'We make to ourselves pictures of facts,' and ending with 3.01, 'The totality of true thoughts is a picture of the world,' the text contains forty *consecutive* entries that deal with the picture theory. The doctrine is picked up again in the entries that follow 4. In that section of the text Wittgenstein says such things as: 'The proposition only asserts something insofar as it is a picture,' 'One name stands for one thing, and another for another thing, and they are connected together. And so the whole, like a living picture, presents the atomic fact.' 'Propositions can be true or false only by being pictures of the reality.' The theory presupposes that in order to be a picture there must be a one-to-one correspondence between the proper names in an elementary proposition and the objects in a corresponding atomic fact. As he writes in 2.13, 'The elements in the picture stand, in the picture, for the objects.'

To obtain an intuitive understanding of what Wittgenstein means by a picture, one might take as a model the relationship between a road map and the terrain it depicts. Such a map has the names of cities arranged in an order corresponding to their relative location on the ground, and it also shows in an exact way the roads that connect them to one another. This mapping relationship is for Wittgenstein a picture. The map is, as it were, a mirror of reality. One might call his view about the relationship of language and the world a 'snap-shot' theory. It is as if language functioned like a photograph of reality. Everything stands still. The idea that language is such a photograph will be abandoned in his later philosophy where the mapping or picturing notion in this sense is rejected. Even in the *Tractatus* Wittgenstein was aware that he was using the word 'picture' in an extended sense, since one would not normally claim that a map is a 'picture', say, of San Diego County. Still because of his adherence to the importance of logic for mirroring the real world, he could not abandon the snap-shot view and in an arresting series of comments defends his usage. Here, beginning with 4.011, are some of the things he says.

> At the first glance the proposition – say as it stands printed on paper – does not seem to be a picture of the reality of which it treats. But nor does the musical score appear at first sight to be a picture of a musical piece; nor does our phonetic spelling (letters) seem to be a picture of our spoken language. And yet these symbolisms prove to be pictures – even in the ordinary sense of the word – of what they represent. It is obvious that we perceive a proposition of the form *aRb* as a picture. Here the sign is obviously a likeness of the signified … The gramophone record, the musical thought, the score, the waves of sound, all stand to one another in that pictorial internal relation, which holds between language and the world. To all of them the logical structure is common.
>
> … In the fact that there is a general rule by which the musician is able to read the symphony out of the score, and that there is a rule by which one could reconstruct the symphony from the line on a gramophone record and from this again – by means of the first rule – construct the score, herein lies the internal similarity between these things which at first sight seem to be entirely different. And the rule is the law of projection which projects the symphony into the language of the musical score. It is the rule of translation of this language into the language of the gramophone record … In order to understand the essence of the proposition, consider hieroglyphic writing, which pictures the facts it describes …

The picture theory is an original and creative conception. It has its faults, to be sure. The elementary proposition 'Smith is tall' does not pick out two objects. The person, Smith, is perhaps an object, but being tall is a property rather than an object. But for a more circumscribed set of correspondences the conception does work. Obviously, the theory depends on assuming that in a formal language, such as *Principia Mathematica,* it is possible to identify elementary propositions and to distinguish them from the propositions in everyday speech with which they might be confused. In essence, then, the theory makes two assumptions: that ordinary language cannot accurately represent reality and that the elementary propositions of a symbolic language can.

The ideal language

But why did Wittgenstein think that everyday language was unsatisfactory for philosophical purposes? And why did he think that by using an ideal language such defects could be overcome? Let us address these questions sequentially.

We begin with a historical point. In 1911, when Wittgenstein was twenty-two, he began a serious study of logic with Russell. Both Frege and Russell deprecated ordinary language. Some of the reasons Wittgenstein gives in the *Tractatus* in defense of this position show their influence; indeed, what he says there might well have been written by his mentors. Both thought that ordinary language is like a mask that conceals the true nature of reality. We thus find Wittgenstein using an elaborate metaphor in 4.002 in which he says that colloquial language 'disguises the thought; so that from the external form of the clothes one cannot infer the form of the thought they clothe, because the external form of the clothes is constructed with quite another object than to let the form of the body be recognized.' Like Frege and Russell, he was also troubled by the problem of non-being, i.e., by the fact that in ordinary speech one can form sentences that seem to treat fictive entities, such as Odysseus and Hamlet, as if they really existed. Frege, for example, says:

> Now, it is a defect of languages that expressions are possible within them, which, in their grammatical form, seemingly determined to designate an object, nevertheless do not fulfill this condition in special cases ... It is to be demanded that in a logically perfect language (logical symbolism) every expression constructed as a proper name in a grammatically correct manner out of already introduced symbols, in fact designate an object; and that no symbol be introduced as a proper name without assurance that it have a nominatum.

In 3.24 Wittgenstein echoes Frege's complaint.

The proposition in which there is mention of a complex, if this does not exist, becomes not nonsense but simply false.

But he also adds other objections:

In the language of everyday life it very often happens that the same word signifies in two different ways – and therefore belongs to two different symbols – or that two words, which signify in different ways, are apparently applied in the same way in the proposition.

In this connection, he specifically mentions ambiguities in the use of 'is.'

Thus the word 'is' appears as the copula, as the sign of equality, and as the expression of existence ... Thus there easily arise the most funda-mental confusions (of which the whole of philosophy is full).

Wittgenstein's solution to these difficulties is to treat philosophi-cal problems by means of an ideal language free of such liabilities. He writes:

In order to avoid these errors, we must employ a symbolism which excludes them, by not applying the same sign in different symbols and by not applying signs in the same way which signify in different ways. A symbolism, that is to say, which obeys the rules of logical grammar – of logical syntax.

(The logical symbolism of Frege and Russell is such a language which, however, does still not exclude all errors.) (3.325)

In the *Tractatus* Wittgenstein does not provide a full-blown descrip-tion of an ideal language. But it is clear that he is referring to the same concept that Frege and Russell developed. Here is Russell's account and the text of the *Tractatus* contains many remarks that closely resemble these:

I propose now to consider what sort of language a logically perfect language would be. In a logically perfect language the words in a proposition would correspond one by one with the components of the corresponding fact, with the exception of such words as 'or,' 'not,' 'if,' 'then,' which have a different function. In a logically perfect language there will be one word and no more for every simple object, and everything that is not simple will be expressed by a combination of words, by a combination derived, of course, from the words for the simple things that enter in, one word for each simple component. A language of that sort will be completely analytic, and will show at a glance the logical structure of the facts asserted or denied. The language which is set forth in *Principia Mathematica* is intended to be a language of that sort … Actual languages are not logically perfect in this sense, and they cannot possibly be, if they are to serve the purposes of daily life.

It will be noted that Russell says that in such a logically perfect language there will be exactly one word for each simple object, and that everything not simple will be expressed by a combination of words derived from those that are simple. But he also asserts that such a language 'will show at a glance the logical structure of the facts asserted or denied.' The textual evidence is overwhelming that Wittgenstein accepted all of these ideas.

As the preceding account makes plain, Logical Atomism is a metaphysical theory. Like many such systems, including those of the idealists, it seeks to give a synoptic account of reality. But unlike most such schemes, those of Wittgenstein and Russell are carefully designed not to advance any theses that are incompatible with the actual or potential findings of science. In his 1924 essay 'Logical Atomism,' Russell says:

> What shall we regard as having the greatest likelihood of being true, and what as proper to be rejected if it conflicts with other evidence? It seems to me that science has a much greater likelihood of being true in the main than any philosophy hitherto advanced (I do not, of course, except my own) … We shall be wise to build our philosophy upon science, because the risk of error in philosophy is pretty sure to be greater than in science … Philosophy should be comprehensive and should be bold in suggesting hypotheses as to the universe which science is not yet in a position to confirm or confute. But these should always be presented *as* hypotheses, not (as is too often done) as immutable certainties like the dogmas of religion.

Wittgenstein is even more forceful.

> The right method of philosophy would be this. To say nothing except what can be said, i.e., the propositions of natural science, i.e., something that has nothing to do with philosophy. (6.53)

How then shall we interpret his Logical Atomism if it purports to be about reality and yet not to be competitive with science? My suggestion is that Wittgenstein thought that there are questions about certain fundamental features of the universe (e.g., whether there are facts, and if so, what their structures are) that are the proper province of metaphysical philosophy. In this respect, the *Tractatus* reminds one of the efforts by Aristotle and Kant to describe the basic categorial features in terms of which all events, processes, and objects can be characterized. Wittgenstein's remark in 6.124 supports this construal. He writes:

> The logical propositions describe the scaffolding of the world, or rather they represent it … They presuppose that names have meaning and that elementary propositions have sense. And this is their connection with the world.

Such approaches are to be distinguished from those of Thales or Empedocles, say, who attempted to depict the fundamental *ingredients of reality,* such as water, earth, air, or fire, rather than the basic categorial features under which all ingredients can be subsumed. It is now clear that they were advancing proto-empirical hypotheses that science later showed to be mistaken. For Wittgenstein, as for Russell, any such task should be left to science. In contrast, it is the fundamental *structural* features of the world that the new logic can uniquely reveal through the opaque mask of ordinary language. Scientific research presupposes the existence of such features but does not and will not investigate them. Thus, as I interpret him, Wittgenstein assumed that there is a descriptive task about reality that uniquely belongs to logic. We can summarize Wittgenstein's Logical Atomism by saying that it is a metaphysical system based on mathematical logic that attempts to provide a non-scientific description of the fundamental structural properties of reality. His great idea about the conditions that significant utterance about the world must satisfy will immediately emerge from such a metaphysics.

The theory of significance

Like many theories, Wittgenstein's about significance – his great idea – is complex and contains multiple elements. In order to explain it with a reasonable degree of fidelity, I shall divide my account into two parts. First, in two paragraphs, I shall summarize it. Following that brief statement I shall deal with its most important ingredients in more detail.

It should be emphasized that this is a theory about *the conditions* that any significant statement about the world must satisfy. It begins with an account of the world. For Wittgenstein there is only one world, the world of nature. The world is the totality of atomic facts – a view that is explained in his Logical Atomism. For Wittgenstein it is propositions rather than names that are the bearers of significance. As he says: 'Names resemble points; propositions resemble arrows, they have sense' (3.144). Not all propositions, notably those of everyday language, describe the atomic facts that comprise the world. Those that do are called 'elementary propositions.' They are a composite of proper names, each of which picks out an object in the world. *An elementary proposition is significant if and only if each of its names denotes a corresponding object arranged in a particular order in an atomic fact.* This is his theory about the conditions for significant utterance. The theory also distinguishes significance from truth. Significance is a necessary condition of truth. An elementary proposition is true if it accurately depicts an atomic fact. It is the factual propositions of science that are true of the world.

Given this picture of the world and the conditions for uttering meaningful sentences about it, Wittgenstein then draws a distinction between what can be said and what can only be shown. His view is that it is only the propositions of the natural sciences that can be said. The world is thus identical with the totality of the atomic facts describable by science. Let us call this his scientism. But that which can be said is to be distinguished from that which can only be shown. The latter cannot be said. Among the things that can only be shown are what Wittgenstein sometimes calls 'values,' sometimes 'the problems of life,' or sometimes 'ethics and aesthetics.' His point is that values do not belong to the natural world. They are not quantifiable, and thus not susceptible to scientific investigation. They can be shown, however. In not belonging to the natural world they are not to be thought of as existing in some other world or realm. There is no other such realm: there is only one world. Insofar as they can be shown they are to be characterized as 'the inexpressible,' 'the transcendental,' or 'the mystical.' It is thus part of Wittgenstein's theory that besides what can be said, i.e., the propositions of science, the inexpressible can be shown. The distinction between science and what can be shown thus leads Wittgenstein to speak about philosophy (or as he sometimes says, 'logic'). His main thesis is that philosophy is not a science but an 'activity.' As such, it cannot make significant or true pronouncements about reality; only science can do so. Therefore, what are its functions? Wittgenstein describes three: two of which are positive, and one negative. The latter occurs when philosophy purports to be a kind of science, when it tries to draw limits to the real world by looking at those limits from 'outside' the world. Since nothing is 'outside' the world – 'The world is everything that is the case' – such accounts are nonsensical. Most of philosophy – especially typical metaphysical theories – are thus nonsense. But philosophy can play two constructive roles. It can engage in the clarification of the propositions of science, and it can sometimes show that which cannot be said. I shall now amplify this summary concentrating on its main subtheses, i.e. its scientism, mysticism, and Wittgenstein's various conceptions of philosophy.

Wittgenstein's scientism

From the earliest historical records we have it is clear that science has always exercised a profound influence on philosophy. But *scientism* must be distinguished from science or from those philosophical theories that merely reflect a scientific influence. Scientism is a special sort of philosophical doctrine. Plato, Aristotle, and Kant take scientific activity seriously but none of them espouses scientism. This view first begins to emerge in the Enlightenment. There is a rudimentary version of it, for example, at the end of Hume's *Enquiry Concerning Human Understanding* (1758). As he says:

> If we take in our hand any volume; of divinity or school metaphysics, for instance; let us ask: *Does it contain any abstract reasoning concerning quantity or number?* No. *Does it contain any experimental reasoning concerning matter of fact and existence?* No. Commit it then to the flames; for it can contain nothing but sophistry and illusion.

I have described Hume's account as 'rudimentary,' since it is less radical than the forms of scientism common in the twentieth century, including one we encounter in the *Tractatus*. The notion that *only* the methods of the natural sciences give rise to true affirmations about reality is today widely accepted in epistemology, metaphysics, philosophy of language, and philosophy of mind. In 1918 in his *General Theory of Knowledge* (*Allgemeine Erkenntnislehre*) Moritz Schlick, the founder of the Vienna Circle, formulated the doctrine in this way: 'Since science in principle can say all that can be said there is no unanswerable question left.' Schlick speaks about what 'can be said.' Wittgenstein also speaks about what can be said.

> The right method of philosophy would be this. To say nothing except what can be said, i.e., the propositions of natural science, i.e., something that has nothing to do with philosophy (6.53).

Somewhat earlier, Charles Sanders Peirce produced another variation on this theme: 'In the idealized long run, the completed science is a true description of reality; there is no other Truth and no other Reality.' But neither Peirce nor Schlick contrasts what can be said with what can be shown. That contrast is drawn only by Wittgenstein.

Hume is more moderate than Peirce or Schlick or, as we shall see, Wittgenstein. Hume is willing to spare abstract reasoning concerning 'quantity and number' from the pyre. It is plausible, therefore, to think that he would have exempted mathematical logic from a similar immolation. But Wittgenstein is tougher minded. He claims that the theorems of logic are tautologies and that tautologies say nothing. 'But all propositions of logic say the same thing. That is nothing' (5.43). His supporting example is memorable: 'I know, e.g., nothing about the weather, when I know that it rains or does not rain' (4.461). Indeed, he asserts that both tautologies and contradictions are without sense, 'like the point from which two arrows go out in opposite directions.'

Moreover, Hume's discussion allows for the possibility of a descriptive role for philosophy if it deals with matters other than 'divinity and school metaphysics.' But Wittgenstein is less charitable. At its most radical, his view is that most philosophical utterances are senseless. He writes:

> Most propositions and questions, that have been written about philosophical matters, are not false, but senseless. We cannot, therefore, answer questions of this kind at all, but only state their senselessness. Most questions and propositions of the philosophers result from the fact that we do not understand the logic of our language.
>
> (They are of the same kind as the question whether the Good is more or less identical than the Beautiful.)
>
> And so it is not to be wondered at that the deepest problems are really *no* problems. (4.003)

Interestingly enough, the *Tractatus* also contains a less harsh assessment of philosophy. This begins with the patently scientistic remark that the totality of true propositions is the total natural science, or the totality of the natural sciences (4.11). Wittgenstein immediately adds that philosophy is not one of the natural sciences 'The word "philosophy" must mean something which stands above or below, but not beside the natural sciences, (4.111). It follows from his scientism that philosophy cannot produce any true propositions. Nevertheless, and surprisingly, he does think philosophy has a positive role to play. As he avers in the next entry:

> The purpose of philosophy is the logical clarification of thoughts. Philosophy is not a theory but an activity.
>
> A philosophical work consists essentially of elucidations.
>
> The result of philosophy is not a number of 'philosophical propositions', but to make propositions clear.
>
> Philosophy should make clear and delimit sharply the thoughts which otherwise are, as it were, opaque and blurred. (4.112)

In each of these five sentences he has managed to pack a quart of information into a pint bottle. The ideas they express are not identical but they are related. Let us try briefly to unpack them, not necessarily in his order.

(i) The purpose of philosophy is the logical clarification of thoughts.

There are three key words in this sentence, 'logical,' 'clarification,' and 'thoughts.' The reference to logic suggests that clarification is possible only in an ideal language. This is because everyday discourse is like a screen that hides the real meaning of thoughts. But a formal language can penetrate the screen and reveal their true nature. Here is an example. Compare: 'Dr. Jekyll is Mr. Hyde,' and 'Dr. Jekyll is the person who drank a chemical potion.' One might think that if Jekyll and Hyde are identical, it would follow, as a matter of logic, that Mr. Hyde drank a chemical potion. But we know from Stevenson's novel that this is false. It was Jekyll who drank the potion that turned him into the monster, Hyde. But then what is wrong with the inference? The answer is that the word 'is' in the sentence 'Dr. Jekyll is Mr. Hyde' is the 'is' of identity, whereas the 'is' in the sentence 'Dr. Jekyll is the person who drank a chemical potion' has a different use; the sentence containing it has to be analyzed according to Russell's theory of descriptions. According to that mathematico-logical theory, 'Dr. Jekyll is the person who drank a chemical potion' is not an identity sentence. Hence, the inference does not go through. Clarification results from logical analysis, and the difference in meaning between the two sentences is brought out perspicuously.

(ii)   Philosophy is not a theory but an activity.

In this sentence Wittgenstein is drawing an opposition between an activity and a theory. We can read him as saying that philosophers should not be in the business of producing theories but doing something else, which he calls 'an activity.' Scientists typically produce theories, such as S. J. Singer's fluid mosaic theory of the cell membrane, or Einstein's general theory of relativity. Most theories consist of 'propositions' that are either true or false. So if philosophers should not be generating theories then what should they be doing?

It is possible that Wittgenstein may have had Socrates in mind in this context. In the Platonic dialogues, Socrates is depicted as wandering around Athens questioning its citizens about all sorts of topics – what they mean by piety, friendship, love, happiness, or the good life. The opening books of the *Republic*, for example, recount a series of such interactions. Socrates asks his acquaintances Cephalus, Polemarcus, Thrasymachus, Glaucon and Adeimantus to explain what justice is. Each sequentially offers a characterization. Cephalus says, for instance, that justice is a matter of honesty in word and deed; it consists in repaying one's debts and in always telling the truth. Socrates points out that this definition is subject to counter-examples. Suppose a madman, with knife in hand, states that he intends to kill a friend of yours and asks where the friend can be found. You know that your friend is innocent of any crime and that the person who intends to murder him is demented. Socrates asks: Would it be just to tell him the truth – to indicate where your friend can be found? It is obvious to Cephalus and the others that it would not; that justice, whatever it means, cannot be identical with telling the truth.

In this verbal interchange, Socrates has not put forth any theory or position of his own. He has simply pointed out that Cephalus' definition is untenable. Furthermore, in his subsequent questioning of the other personages, he follows the same procedure. They put forth fixed views and he finds counter-instances to each of them. It becomes increasingly clear that none of their characterizations will do. We can describe what Socrates is doing as an activity. He is engaging his interlocutors in an ongoing dialogue about the meaning of a certain concept. Unlike those who have settled opinions, Socrates remains open-minded. His only commitment is to the investigative process itself. In the early Platonic dialogues this mode of inquiry fails to arrive at any settled results, but this does not seem to bother Socrates. One has the sense that for Socrates the activity of interrogation is almost an end in itself. In his later philosophy Wittgenstein says that what is important for him is not that he has achieved certain results but that he has developed a new method for doing philosophy. My suggestion is that this idea is prefigured in the *Tractatus* and it may be that this work can be interpreted as a specimen of the kind of activity he thinks philosophers should engage in.

(iii) The result of philosophy is not a number of 'philosophical propositions,' but to make propositions clear.

(iv) Philosophy should make clear and delimit sharply the thoughts which otherwise are, as it were, opaque and blurred.

If philosophy is, or should be, an activity, what is its point or purpose? What is supposed to be the outcome of the activity? Wittgenstein answers that it should make propositions and thoughts clear. This is what Socrates is also trying to do. We can see from his counter-examples that those who put forth theses or doctrines do not have clear thoughts. His dialectical method seems to imply that if they were able to formulate a thesis that is impervious to counter-instances their thoughts would be clear. The activity that Socrates is engaging in is thus designed to help his interlocutors achieve clarity. But note: his is not an empirical inquiry but a conceptual one. He is not amassing or citing experimental data. He is simply asking his fellow citizens, as native speakers of a natural language, to think more deeply about what they mean by what they say. His counter-examples are key moves in producing such self-criticism. We can infer from Socrates' practice that he believes that his insistent questioning should lead to clarity. So his quest is, in Wittgenstein's parlance, 'to make clear and delimit sharply the thoughts which otherwise are, as it were, opaque and blurred.'

(v) A philosophical work consists essentially of elucidations.

I take it that by using the locution 'elucidations', Wittgenstein is not merely repeating what he said in (iii) and (iv) above. In other words it is sensible to presuppose that he wishes to differentiate the concept of an *elucidation* from that of *making thoughts clear*. One might think that these notions are synonymous, and hence that he is simply producing a terminological variation on what he had previously said. I do not think that this is the case. The *Oxford English Dictionary* supports this interpretation. Although the term 'elucidation' has several meanings, its main sense, according to the dictionary, is that it is an explanation. It is true, of course, that an explanation is designed to clarify something, but there are ways other than the Socratic approach for doing so. Thus, one can speak of the elucidation of the chemical structure of an antibiotic. Such an elucidation would involve a process entirely different from the dialectical method followed by Socrates. Accordingly, when Wittgenstein says that a philosophical work consists essentially of elucidations, I think he is speaking about explanations. It is interesting that in 6.54 Wittgenstein sums up what he has done in the *Tractatus* as 'elucidatory.' We shall see below what it is that he wished to explain in writing this book.

Wittgenstein's scientism is thus ambivalent about the value of philosophy. It denigrates metaphysics but grants legitimacy to a kind of activity that leads to clarification and elucidation. A third, positive conception of philosophy is connected with the inexpressible and the transcendental. But before making this explicit we must deal with his mysticism and the concepts of saying and showing on which it is based. This conception of philosophy is also closely connected to his great idea.

Wittgenstein's mysticism

The *Tractatus* is notable for the many contrasts it draws in its seventy-nine pages. It distinguishes elementary propositions from atomic facts, the world from the language humans use to talk about it, facts from objects, names from propositions, science from philosophy, and so forth. But arguably the most important such distinction is that between saying and showing. Almost all of the other contrasts follow from it. It is also the source of his account of the mystical. As he says: 'There is indeed the inexpressible. This *shows* itself; it is the mystical' (6.522). In the Preface Wittgenstein states that the whole meaning of the book can be summarized in two statements: *What can be said at all can be said clearly*; and *Whereof one cannot speak, thereof one must be silent.* So the distinction between what can be said and what cannot be said takes us to the heart of the *Tractatus*.

But what exactly is the distinction? Given its importance, I find it puzzling that Wittgenstein nowhere expatiates on these two notions. In 4.1212 he writes: 'What *can* be shown *cannot* be said.' If we take this utterance literally he is drawing an opposition between showing and saying. If something can be shown it cannot be said and, presumably, if it can be said it cannot be shown. Still, he does offer the reader two pieces of helpful information for understanding the distinction.

First, he asserts that the only things that can be said are the propositions of natural science (6.53). But he remains silent about why this is so. It seems to be a presupposition rather than a position supported by argument. Second, he mentions many things that can *only* be shown. Solipsism is one of them. 'In fact what solipsism *means*, is quite correct, only it cannot be *said*, but it shows itself' (5.62). The existence of a thinking, willing self can only be shown. In 5.641 he states: 'The philosophical I is not the man, not the human body or the human soul of which psychology treats, but the metaphysical subject, the limit – not part of the world.' In saying these things are 'not part of the world,' he should be interpreted as meaning that they are not part of the world of nature. For this reason, values (including ethics and aesthetics) are not susceptible to scientific inquiry. As he writes in a series of passages:

> The sense of the world must lie outside the world. In the world everything is as it is and happens as it does happen. *In* it there is no value – and if there were, it would be of no value. If there is a value which is of value, it must lie outside all happening and being-so. For all happening and being-so is accidental.
>
> What makes it non-accidental cannot lie in the world, for otherwise this would again be accidental. It must lie outside the world. (6.41)

> Hence, also there can be no ethical propositions. Propositions cannot express anything higher. (6.42)

> It is clear that ethics cannot be expressed.
> Ethics is transcendental.
> (Ethics and aesthetics are one.) (6.421)

Wittgenstein does offer an extensive explanation about why some things can only be shown. To grasp his meaning, let us return to the early sections of the *Tractatus*. As I pointed out earlier, they contain a metaphysical theory about the relationship between language and the world. The question the theory is designed to answer is: 'How is it possible that by uttering a series of noises or writing down a series of marks on paper a person can say something about the world or communicate with others?' As I pointed out above, Wittgenstein's answer, somewhat oversimplified, is the famous Picture Theory.

However, sometimes instead of speaking of a picture, Wittgenstein speaks of a *representation*. Using this locution, he will say that an elementary proposition *represents* an atomic fact. It does so because there is an exact correspondence between its structure and the structure of an atomic fact, i.e., there is a mirroring relationship between the arrangement that proper names bear to each other in the proposition, and the arrangement that the objects bear to one another in the fact. When the elementary proposition is meaningful and true it pictures that correspondence. This is his theory of significance. But Wittgenstein adds another dimension to the account. He says that representation or picturing is possible only if the elementary proposition and the ingredients of the world share the same logical form. This common feature – i.e., the common logical form they share – cannot itself be represented in language. It is a tertium quid, neither a fact nor an elementary proposition. It can therefore only be shown. He thus advances a general argument here about the limits of what language can say. From this argument he concludes that there are things that can only be shown.

Put somewhat differently, his contention is that elementary propositions can represent reality but they cannot *say* what they must have in common with reality in order to represent it. This common feature he calls 'the logical form of the proposition.' It can only be shown, because in order to say what it is, 'we should have to put ourselves with the propositions outside logic, that is outside the world.' And this is impossible since there is nothing outside the world. Wittgenstein expands on this theme by asserting 'that which mirrors itself in language language cannot represent, and that which expresses *itself* in language *we* cannot express by language. The propositions *show* the logical form of reality. They exhibit it' (4.121). Here we find a view of philosophy that is positive. Logic shows the structure of the world but cannot express what it shows. Nonetheless, in mirroring itself in language it is showing something important about the world that cannot be captured by science. What can only be shown transcends the limits of the natural world, and thus transcends science. This he designates as 'the mystical.'

These passages suggest that Wittgenstein is giving a description of the limits of the natural world and of what lies beyond it. If one were to interpret him in this way it would seem that he is a kind of Kantian. Kant's central aim was to describe the limits of what can be known: this he terms the 'phenomenal world.' It is a domain defined by the categories of space and time. But Kant is sometimes interpreted as holding that the knowable world has an external, unknowable cause, a realm he nominates as the 'noumenal.'

Whether this is a correct rendering of Kant has been widely disputed, but it is probably the standard interpretation. On this interpretation, Wittgenstein's project in the *Tractatus* would be assimilated to Kant's. The difference would be that Kant's concern is with epistemology, i.e., with the conditions that must be satisfied in order to obtain knowledge of the external world, and Wittgenstein's with ontology, i.e., with what the structure of the world is like and how it is possible to say anything significant about it. On that reading it would follow that Wittgenstein, like Kant, is committed to a doctrine of two worlds. Science speaks about one of them and cannot speak about the other. The mystical transcends science, and is the realm occupied by values, the human psyche, and whatever is inexpressible. On this construal, one of the main tasks of the *Tractatus* is to define the limits of what is sayable, and that limit is found to be identical with what the physical sciences can in principle investigate.

There are passages in the book that seem to support such an interpretation. Consider the following:

Philosophy limits the disputable sphere of natural science (4.113).
It should limit the thinkable and thereby the unthinkable.
It should limit the unthinkable from within through the thinkable (4.114).
It will mean the unspeakable by clearly displaying the speakable (4.115).

In saying that philosophy should limit the thinkable and unthinkable, and that it should limit the unthinkable from within through the thinkable, these citations seem to be suggesting that philosophy has a special kind of authority, one that exercises itself by drawing limits between two separate domains. The citations thus imply that Wittgenstein is committed to a two-worlds doctrine somewhat similar to that we find in Kant. But a more careful analysis shows that it is precisely this Kantian interpretation that he is rejecting.

In the Preface, for instance, he explains that it is impossible to think both sides of this limit and indeed that what lies on the other side is simply nonsense. Insofar as philosophy tries to draw such a limit it is a species of nonsense. Here is what he writes there:

> This book will, therefore, draw a limit to thinking, or rather – not to thinking, but to the expression of thoughts; for, in order to draw a limit to thinking we should have to be able to think both sides of this limit (we should therefore have to be able to think what cannot be thought).
>
> The limit can, therefore, only be drawn in language and what lies on the other side of the limit will be simply nonsense.

Within the text we find similar passages.

> Logic fills the world: the limits of the world are also its limits.
>
> We cannot therefore say in logic: This and this there is in the world, that there is not.
>
> For that would apparently presuppose that we exclude certain possibilities, and this cannot be the case since otherwise logic must get outside the limits of the world: that is, if it could consider these limits from the other side also.
>
> What we cannot think, that we cannot think: we cannot therefore *say* what we cannot think (5.61).

It is clear from these remarks that Wittgenstein is denying that we can survey the speakable from a position outside the speakable. Logic cannot get outside the limits of the world. And if not, then we cannot think about the limits from 'the other side,' since nothing exists beyond those limits. It follows that if we cannot think certain things we cannot say them either. Therefore, since the mystical does not exist within the natural world we cannot say anything about it. But it can be shown and this a function that philosophy (logic) may perform. The doctrine of showing is accordingly not a theory about the metaphysical powers or capacities of philosophy. Because metaphysics seeks a perspective outside of the world from which to draw the limits of the world, and thus to say something about the mystical, he concludes that its propositions are nonsense. That is what he is telling us when he writes: 'What we cannot think, that we cannot think; we cannot therefore *say* what we cannot think.'

The *Tractatus* itself

In the opening chapter of this book I stated that Wittgenstein was virtually unique among the many distinguished cultural figures of the Western tradition in having had three great ideas. In the preceding eight sections of this chapter I tried to explain what the earliest of those ideas was, and my contention was that it consisted of a theory about the conditions that must be satisfied if significant utterance about the world is possible. This idea, I claimed, was embedded in the *Tractatus Logico-Philosophicus* of 1922, the only book that Wittgenstein published in his lifetime. But now it is important to draw a distinction between that great idea and the *Tractatus* itself. In other words, I am saying that to have identified his unique idea is not to have explained what the *Tractatus* itself is about. There is much more to the book than the theory of significance that it contains. In concluding this chapter, therefore, I would like to give the reader some sense of the *Tractatus* itself.

It should be said at the outset that it is one of the most difficult philosophical texts of the century. Perhaps the best word for it is *enigmatic*. It is only seventy-nine pages long and consists of 525 short affirmations, most of them aphorisms, and many no longer than a sentence or two. Each of these is numbered in an unusual arrangement that I will explain below. Each is a compact, often enigmatic saying. One might suggest – borrowing a metaphor from the later Wittgenstein – that in each of them the author has condensed a cloud of philosophy into a drop of grammar. Many of these are thus hard to unravel and taken as a group they are susceptible to various interpretations. The general effect they make upon the reader is that the text is a kind of cryptogram that requires deciphering. In part this is because many of its sentences are composed of technical words, including logical symbols based on the notation of *Principia Mathematica* and occasionally some non-standard symbols invented by Wittgenstein himself. The original German contains several locutions that are difficult to render into English. In German they are often used as synonyms but Wittgenstein sharply differentiates them for technical purposes. Stylistically it is so odd that its first translator, C. K. Ogden, felt obliged to explain why the printed book takes the form it does.

> In rendering Mr. Wittgenstein's *Tractatus Logico-Philosophicus* available for English readers, the somewhat unusual course has been adopted of printing the original side by side with the translation. Such a method of presentation seemed desirable both on account of the obvious difficulties raised by the vocabulary and in view of the peculiar literary character of the whole. As a result, a certain latitude has been possible in passages to which objection might otherwise be taken as over-literal.

As far as I know, no other philosophical book before the *Tractatus* was printed in this fashion, with facing pages of the German text on one side and the English translation on the other. Ogden explains that he decided on this unusual form of presentation both because of its special vocabulary and what he describes as 'the peculiar literary character of the whole.' Because of these remarkable features, I doubt that any intelligent person could make head or tail of it on a first reading. Indeed, even graduate students and professional philosophers who are not steeped in the work of Frege and Russell would have similar difficulties.

There is a second set of difficulties of a literary sort. The book does not look like a typical philosophical work. It is not discursive and does not begin with a statement of its central thesis or main theme. Indeed, the only such statement, three lines in length, appears in its Preface. There are no other guidelines. It is not divided into chapters and contains almost no arguments. The original manuscript had no index (the index in the Ogden translation was supplied by Max Black), no bibliography, no reference to works cited, a two-page Preface in which he acknowledges the influences of Frege and Russell, and it contains only two footnotes, one by Wittgenstein himself on its first page and one inserted later by Russell to explain entry 6.32.

Third, there are difficulties about its contents. In several places it looks as if Wittgenstein is contradicting himself or taking back things he says elsewhere. Here are three examples.

1. Wittgenstein's footnote on page 1 is important because in it he describes the function of the numbering system. He indicates that the system is designed to exhibit the relative importance of the aphorisms (or propositions) in the work. Thus, those having single numbers (e.g., 1, 2, 3 etc.) are the most important. Multiple-numbered propositions are expansions of or comments on those with single numbers. Here, as an illustration, are the first eight propositions of the *Tractatus*.

1.   The world is everything that is the case.
1.1   The world is the totality of facts, not of things.
1.11 The world is determined by the facts, and these being *all* the facts.
1.12 For the totality of facts determines both what is the case, and also all that is not the case.
1.13 The facts in logical space are the world.
1.2   The world divides into facts.
1.21 Anyone can either be the case or not be the case, and everything else remains the same.
2.   What is the case, the fact, is the existence of atomic facts.

According to the footnote, the propositions numbered 1 and 2 in the above list are the most important. Those numbered 1.1 and 1.2 are less important; they are comments on proposition 1. Those numbered 1.11, 1.12, and 1.13 are still less important; they are comments on the proposition that immediately precedes them. That is, 1.11 is a comment on 1.1, 1.12 is a comment on 1.11, 1.13 is a comment on 1.12, and so on.

Following these rules, we should be able to elicit the fundamental structure of the work by listing all those propositions having single natural numbers. There are seven of these.

1. The world is everything that is the case.
2. What is the case, the fact, is the existence of atomic facts.
3. The logical picture of the facts is the thought.
4. The thought is the significant proposition.
5. Propositions are truth-functions of elementary propositions. (An elementary proposition is a truth-function of itself.)
6. The general form of truth-function is: $[\bar{p}, \bar{\xi}, N(\bar{\xi})]$. This is the general form of proposition.
7. Whereof one cannot speak, thereof one must be silent.

However, if we study this group of statements it is difficult to find an interpretation that links all of them. The first six propositions are related. They fall into connected pairs, and it is not difficult to follow the train of ideas that begins with 1 and ends with 6. Thus, 1 states that the world is everything that is the case, and 2 picks up the reference to what is the case, adding that what is the case is the existence of atomic facts. 3 is connected with 2 through the word 'fact.' It states that the logical picture of the facts is the thought. And 4 expands on this proposition by stating that the thought is the significant proposition. 5 is tied to 4 in referring to propositions; it asserts that they are truth functions of elementary propositions and 6 continues the reference to propositions by describing the general form of truth-functions or propositions. But the transition from 6 to 7 is puzzling. The two propositions do not seem logically connected at all. There seems to be no interpretation of 7 that fits it into the six preceding propositions. We have thus arrived at one of the work's 'peculiar' features. Its numbering system is presumably designed to give the reader a picture of its basic conceptual structure; yet the system of numbers does not (at least prima facie) provide such a coherent thesis.

2. Apart from this problem, the numbering system seems to be inconsistent with what Wittgenstein declares the book to be about. In its brief Preface, he says:

> The book deals with the problems of philosophy and shows, as I believe, that the method of formulating these problems rests on the misunderstanding of the logic of our language. Its whole meaning could be summed up somewhat as follows: What can be said at all

can be said clearly; and whereof one cannot speak thereof one must
be silent.

In this passage Wittgenstein is explaining what 'the whole meaning'
of the book is. He summarizes it in two statements: (1) What can be
said at all can be said clearly, and (2) Whereof one cannot speak
thereof one must be silent.

At least two puzzles arise in the light of these remarks. First, it
will be noted that the second of the two statements is identical
with proposition 7 in our list of fundamental propositions. But if
the whole meaning of the book is identical with what proposition
7, and the proposition that what can be said at all can be said
clearly, state, then what is the relevance of the propositions
numbered 1 through 6 that we adumbrated above? Are they no
longer what the whole meaning of the book is about? Second, it
will be noted that the proposition 'What can be said at all can be
said clearly' is not in the list of the seven propositions described by
single natural numbers. Where does it come from, and why is it
suddenly given such important status? Its status raises complexities we cannot explore here. But the answer to where it comes from
is comparatively simple. We find that entry 4.116 in the text reads
as follows:

Everything that can be thought at all can be thought clearly.
Everything that can be said can be said clearly.

It seems that 'What can be said at all can be said clearly' is a variation
on 4.116. But according to the numbering system this is a comparatively unimportant proposition. It is a direct comment on 4.115,
which says:

It will mean the unspeakable by clearly displaying the speakable.

Still, if we follow the rules of the numbering system, 4.116 is a
comparatively insignificant statement. It is an indirect comment, of
course, on 4, i.e., the proposition 'The thought is the significant
proposition.' But 4.116 stands forty-seventh in the list of entries that
follow 4. It is thus difficult to see how it can be as important as
Wittgenstein says it is in the Preface.

3. I turn now to the last and most important of these difficulties. In the Tractatus Wittgenstein seems committed to three major views, Logical Atomism, Scientism, and Mysticism. These seem to be incompatible with one another. Logical Atomism is a metaphysical system about the structure of reality. Scientism tells us that any such system is nonsense, since it is only the propositions of science that can say anything that is both significant and true about the world, including its structure. Mysticism suggests that values, the metaphysical ego, and the problems of life do not exist in nature. Yet Scientism tells us that there is nothing existing outside of nature. Is it possible to arrive at an interpretation of the Tractatus that can establish that these apparently contradictory views are not really incompatible? I wish to suggest – admittedly with some degree of trepidation – that we can find such a solution. It derives from what Wittgenstein says in the famous ladder metaphor in the penultimate entry of the work. I quote the passage in its entirety.

> My propositions are elucidatory in this way: he who understands me finally recognizes them as senseless, when he has climbed out through them, on them, over them. (He must so to speak throw away the ladder, after he has climbed up on it.)
>
> He must surmount these propositions; then he sees the world rightly (6.54).

As we saw earlier, Wittgenstein asserted that all philosophical conceits are nonsensical because they seek to do that which is logically impossible, i.e., to draw limits to the world from a point of view which is outside of it. In entry 6.54 he seems to be stating that the propositions he himself has uttered in this work and that constitute his Logical Atomism, Scientism, and Mysticism are all guilty of this fault. Each doctrine in its own way attempts to set limits to the world and thus each is senseless. The essential message of the *Tractatus* is thus a rejection of all such views. This is the point of the ladder metaphor.

He begins the passage by saying that his propositions are elucidatory. As we have seen, an elucidation is an explanation. He is therefore offering an explanation here. The explanation is that his readers should treat the propositions in the *Tractatus* as a bridge for understanding *him*. What he is now saying is not senseless. He is sending a message. That message is neither a philosophical proposition nor a proposition of science. It is something like an appeal. He is urging his readers to change their orientation to the world, in particular recommending that they overcome the disposition to see the world through the lens of philosophy. There is an autobiographical tinge suggested in this passage. In effect, it contains a mea culpa. He is implying that his readers will only understand that philosophical propositions are senseless when they have done what he has done, namely 'climbed out through them, on them, over them.' Wittgenstein's message is that one cannot see the world as it is unless one has first been captured by philosophy and then has climbed through and and over its propositions. Part of what it is to see the world rightly is to see that philosophy is nonsense. The rest is to remain silent about what cannot be said. His message thus describes a series of developmental phases for an intelligent human being. There is first the deep conviction that a theory is right. There is second the realization that it makes no sense. There is finally the awareness that this is true of all philosophical doctrines.

In the case of the *Tractatus* the theory that captured Wittgenstein was Logical Atomism, with its emphasis upon an ideal language. That emphasis he inherited from Frege and Russell. Deepening their views, he became convinced that the new logic had momentous consequences for understanding the structure of reality. The opening sections of the *Tractatus* are written under the influence of that compelling idea. But it was only by working *through* that theory that he was able to realize that it was senseless. Wittgenstein states that only when one has reached this level of maturity can one throw away the (philosophical) ladder. And then one will see the world rightly.

The *Tractatus* is a work composed at various stages and under various influences, including the effect the First World War had on Wittgenstein. But its final message is a new and original view about the nature of philosophy. From this perspective it follows that the three apparently contradictory views, Logical Atomism, Scientism, and Mysticism are not incompatible. That is because all are equally nonsensical, and specimens of nonsense cannot be logically inconsistent. In the final sentences of the Preface Wittgenstein states: 'I am, therefore, of the opinion that the problems have in essentials been finally solved. And if I am not mistaken in this, then the value of the work secondly consists in the fact that it shows how little has been done when these problems have been solved.' Wittgenstein is saying that all philosophical problems have been solved. They have been solved by showing that all such problems are really no problems at all. The philosophical propositions that create them are nonsensical. The problems are solved by showing that this is so. And that is what he has done in the *Tractatus*.

Proposition 7 – 'Whereof one cannot speak, thereof one must be silent' – can now be seen to be as important as the Preface tells us it is. It is a distillation of the main message of the *Tractatus*: that one cannot do philosophy because one cannot do what it requires: to think and say that which cannot be thought and therefore cannot be said.

Philosophical Investigations

Introduction

As we saw in Chapter 1, Wittgenstein's views about the nature of philosophy were moving in new directions even before he returned to Cambridge in 1929. Carnap noted some of these changes when he first encountered Wittgenstein in 1927, but immersed in the *Tractatus*, he did not fully appreciate their significance. Those burgeoning ideas were to solidify in the years 1930–1933. In that period Wittgenstein worked out a new method for doing philosophy that led him to reject the logico-mathematical approach of the *Tractatus*, and nearly all of its central theses: that ordinary language is defective and conceals the nature of reality, that some things can only be shown and not said, that science alone can make meaningful statements about the world, and that all philosophical 'propositions' are nonsensical. This method was his second great idea. It stands in striking contrast to the insight that motivated the writing of the *Tractatus*. Indeed, it is something entirely new in the history of philosophy. His remark in *Philosophical Investigations* (66), 'Don't think, but look!' expresses this idea in a compact form. There are several variations on it. 'Don't say: "There must be something common, or they would not be called 'games'" – but look and see whether there is anything common to all' (66).

Earlier in that work he had written: 'In order to see more clearly, here as in countless similar cases, we must focus on the details of what goes on; must look at them *from close to*' (50). The contrast between thinking and looking closely is even carried over to his final notebook, *On Certainty*.

> If, e.g. someone says: 'I don't know if there's a hand here' he might be told 'Look closer.' This possibility of satisfying oneself is part of the language-game. It is one of its essential features. (3)

All the distinctive doctrines of the later philosophy flow from the idea *Don't think, but look!* These include the concept of a language game, the doctrine of family resemblance, the notion that we must replace explanation by description, the emphasis on examples and intermediate cases, and the view that philosophy consists of a series of reminders. The new idea even affected Wittgenstein's literary style. Instead of the laconic remarks that make up the *Tractatus*, his writing in the *Investigations* is looser and flows. The style mirrors the content. He points out in the Preface that it is

> connected with the very nature of the investigation. For this compels us to travel over a wide field of thought criss-cross in every direction. The philosophical remarks in this book are, as it were, a number of sketches of landscapes, which were made in the course of these long and involved journeys.

These, of course, are sketches of conceptual, not topographical, landscapes. They are designed to uncover the profound intellectual and linguistic models that are the sources of philosophical perplexity, and to show by way of contrast how *looking closely* can help us understand and resolve these difficulties.

Unfortunately, Wittgenstein does not explain what the new method is; he assumes that the reader will pick it up in the course of reading his work. In fact, the method is complex and not easy to explain. This is because it is evinced in an aphoristic style that I call 'the broken text.' It is marked by the quasi-Socratic device of posing questions and often leaving them hanging and unanswered. Even some of the aphorisms that take the form of assertions can be thought of as implicit queries, as if they should finish with a question mark. The same topics are discussed over and over again, looked at from this perspective and from that. As he remarks in the Preface:

> The same or almost the same points were always being approached afresh from different directions, and new sketches made. Very many of these were badly drawn or uncharacteristic, marked by all the defects of a weak draughtsman. And when they were rejected a number of tolerable ones were left, which now had to be arranged, and sometimes cut down, so that if you looked at them you could get a picture of the landscape. Thus, this book is really only an album.

What the reader is exposed to is thus a kaleidoscopic investigative process that does not take the form of explicit argumentation leading to the sorts of definitive conclusions that traditional philosophy has aimed at. As Wittgenstein says, 'If one tried to advance theses in philosophy, it would never be possible to debate them, because everyone would agree to them' (*Philosophical Investigations*, 128). Furthermore, there are no summaries of earlier sections or signposts as to where one stands at that moment in the text. It is dubious that the process has anything that could be called an end. In that respect it resembles the inquiries of the early Socrates.

What then is the point of the method? The answer is two-fold: it has both a positive and a negative purpose. With respect to its negative function he makes such comments as: 'Where does our investigation get its importance from, since it seems only to destroy everything interesting, that is, all that is great and important? (As it were all the buildings, leaving behind only bits of stone and rubble.) What we are destroying is nothing but houses of cards and we are clearing up the ground of language on which they stand' (118). 'The results of philosophy are the uncovering of one or another piece of plain nonsense and of bumps that the understanding has got by running its head up against the limits of language. These bumps make us see the value of the discovery' (119). 'The problems are solved, not by giving new information, but by arranging what we have always known. Philosophy is a battle against the bewitchment of our intelligence by means of language' (109). 'A main source of our failure to understand is that we do not *command a clear view* of the use of our words' (122). Such remarks seem to echo comments in the *Tractatus*, where he writes:

> Most questions and propositions of the philosophers result from the fact that we do not understand the logic of our language (4.003).

However, these similar-sounding apothegms are supported by entirely different reasons. What Wittgenstein means in the *Investigations* by 'our failure to understand is that we do not *command a clear view* of the use of our words' is not what he means in the *Tractatus* when he says 'we do not understand the logic of our language.' Though he speaks in both cases about how misunderstanding the role of language can lead to philosophical perplexity, the similarities are more apparent than real, as we shall see below.

There is a second, positive thrust to the method. It also sounds like something he says in the *Tractatus*. There he states that anyone who understands that work will eventually see the world rightly. In the *Investigations* he speaks of obtaining a 'perspicuous representation' of things. In both books Wittgenstein is saying that the new method will allow a person to see the world as it really is. The notion of *seeing* is crucial in both texts. But *what* one will see in following the method of the *Investigations* is not what one would see if one followed the method of the *Tractatus*. One would not be apprehending pictures of atomic propositions. The positive point of the new method – the purpose of focusing on the details of what goes on – is surprising. It is to 'leave everything as it is.' This is a highly provocative statement and will require some unravelling to grasp what it means and why it is important.

Wittgenstein's conception of philosophy

Before we can understand his new method, it is necessary to stand back from the detailed analyses we find in his later texts and look at two presuppositions that underlie his entire approach to philosophy. In effect, we are asking: Is there a continuity in his thinking from the time of his undergraduate studies with Russell in 1911–1913 to his final writings in 1951 about the nature, purpose,

and limits of this discipline? My answer is that there is. This statement is consistent with maintaining that during his career there
were radical developments in his outlook. His three different great
ideas – as expressed successively in the *Tractatus*, the *Philosophical
Investigations*, and *On Certainty* – never reject these fundamental
presuppositions, which are constants that underlie the developing
transformations in his thought.

In their barest forms the two presuppositions are: (1) The aim of
philosophy is to give a correct description and thus to arrive at an
accurate understanding of the world, and (2) Such a description is
not scientific in character. Or to put this last point in a somewhat
different way: Philosophy is not a science. Wittgenstein's view is that
philosophy is an autonomous discipline. It has a unique set of problems and its approach to them differs from that of any other
academic or scholarly inquiry. Philosophy is not history, literature,
linguistics, or psychology, and, of course, it is not any kind of
science.

It follows from the conjunction of these presuppositions that the
methodology and results of philosophical inquiry cannot be identical with those of science. In the *Tractatus* mathematical logic is the
methodology. It describes the world as composed of atomic facts
and their constituents. In *Philosophical Investigations* and in *On
Certainty* both the Tractarian methodology and its findings are
rejected. They are replaced by a methodology that appeals to everyday discourse. Its aim is accurately to describe certain features of
everyday life. Thus in each of these later works his philosophy
continues to be devoted to describing 'what goes on.' Hence,
Wittgenstein's entire philosophy, from its earliest to its final days,
can be thought of as responding to the challenge: *If philosophy is not
a science, what can it tell us about reality?* His new method is the final
device he uses for responding to this challenge. 'A perspicuous
representation,' he says, 'produces just that understanding which
consists in "seeing connexions." Hence, the importance of finding
and inventing intermediate cases' (122).

The textual evidence for the existence of the second presupposition is abundant. Here are some samples.

Philosophy is not one of the natural sciences.

(The word 'philosophy' must mean something which stands above or below, but not beside the natural sciences.) (*Tractatus*, 4.111)

It was true to say that our considerations could not be scientific ones. It was not of any possible interest to us to find out empirically 'that contrary to our preconceived ideas, it is possible to think such-and-such' whatever that may mean. (*Philosophical Investigations*, 109)

Someone who doubted whether the earth had existed for 100 years might have a scientific, or on the other hand a philosophical, doubt. (*On Certainty*, 259)

The evidence is equally strong for the presupposition that the task of philosophy is descriptive. We have already seen in the previous chapter that the *Tractatus* contains a metaphysics dedicated to giving an accurate description of certain structural features of the world. In the *Investigations* Wittgenstein says: 'We must do away with all *explanation*, and description alone must take its place' (109). But in this work his descriptive approach is not a form of metaphysics. *On Certainty* describes a background that is presupposed by everyone in daily life, but which is so obvious as not to be noticed. In that work his aim is bifurcated: it is to describe both certain aspects of everyday life – those activities which he sometimes calls 'the language game' and sometimes 'a form of life' – and a background that everyday life presupposes. The background is identified with certainty. Unlike a scientific theory or historical conjecture, it is not revisable or eliminable. The existence of the earth, for example, is part of that background, and is presupposed, for example, by any scientific or historical investigation. As he says, 'it is just there like your life.' His description of this background consists of a series of graphic metaphors: it is *bedrock, the scaffolding of our thoughts, that which stands fast for all of us, rock bottom, the substratum of all my inquiring, unmoving foundations*, etc.

There is no doubt that Wittgenstein is a highly original thinker. Yet his descriptive method is, in an important sense, traditional. He is doing something that the pre-Socratics would have found congenial. Many of these early philosophers, Thales, Anaximander, Heraclitus, and Democritus, were interested in giving an accurate account of reality. Their methods and their results were primitive by today's sophisticated standards; but the notion that philosophy can and should describe the world is a presupposition they share with Wittgenstein. But having said that, one must also stress that Wittgenstein's method is wholly different from anything we find in any writer before him.

In bringing out the fundamental importance of that method, I shall concentrate on four of its features: first, its intimate connection with his conception of the nature of philosophy; second, its manifestation in a special literary style that, as previously mentioned, I call 'the broken text;' third, its emphasis on examples and particular cases and their connection with 'the language game;' and finally, its purpose or aim, i.e., what Wittgenstein hopes to accomplish by its use. I begin with his conception of philosophy.

Wittgenstein's most sustained metadiscussion of the nature of philosophy and its problems is to be found in the *Investigations*, from approximately entry 89 to 133, i.e., in about nine pages of text. Those nine pages are extremely concentrated; one could easily devote a book to them. We shall restrict our discussion to a few salient points.

In these pages Wittgenstein uses the term 'philosophy' in two different ways. In one of these uses he is referring to what might be called traditional philosophy. Philosophy, on this interpretation, is a conceptual activity which attempts, in non-scientific, non-empirical ways, to understand the nature of the world and the beings that inhabit it. It attempts to facilitate such an understanding by finding underlying principles and patterns in what seems to be a confusing flux of events and happenings. There is thus a similarity of aim between it and science. The scientist connects up such differing phenomena as the movement of the tides, the falling of an apple from a tree, and the fact that the moon does not plunge into the earth, by discovering a 'hidden' principle, the law of gravitation, in terms of which all these events are explained. Such principles are not to be found in surface phenomena; if they were they could be discerned by anyone. Rather they are deep-lying, hidden beneath the diversity of the phenomena and activities we all experience in daily life. So, not unlike science, traditional philosophy engages in a quest to uncover the hidden, the essences of things, the covert principles that will allow us to make sense of the world as we find it. 'We feel,' Wittgenstein writes, 'as if we had to penetrate phenomena', and about the philosopher's quest for the essence and the hidden he says:

> For they see in the essence, not something that already lies open to view and that becomes surveyable by a rearrangement, but some- thing that lies beneath the surface. Something that lies within, which we see when we look into the thing, and which an analysis digs out.
>   'The essence is hidden from us'; this is the form our problem now assumes. (*Philosophical Investigations*, 92)

In contrast to this traditional outlook, Wittgenstein agues that nothing of philosophical interest is hidden. On the contrary every- thing lies open to view; but traditional practitioners must be reminded of that fact; this is why they must look more closely at everyday activity. He says: 'Since everything lies open to view there is nothing to explain' (126). 'The aspects of things that are most important for us are hidden because of their simplicity and famil- iarity. (One is unable to notice something – because it is always before one's eyes.)' (129) That is why the work of the descriptive philosopher 'consists in assembling reminders for a particular purpose' (127). Nonetheless, for Wittgenstein, traditional philoso- phy is doing something interesting and important, something that has the character of depth. It is profound in its attempt to discover the basic principles of reality. And the problems themselves are profound. As he puts it, this is an activity which gives rise to 'deep disquietudes.' Its problems have roots that are 'as deep in us as the forms of our language and their significance is as great as the importance of our language.' As can be seen from the attitudes he is expressing here, Wittgenstein does not disparage traditional philos- ophy. He respects it and the stubborn problems it is attempting to solve. His attitude is thus completely different from that of such logical positivists as A. J. Ayer who asserted that 'The traditional disputes of philosophers are, for the most part, as unwarranted as they are unfruitful.' (*Language, Truth, and Logic*, Ch. I)

Wittgenstein's main criticism of traditional philosophy is that it does not so much discover patterns in reality as attempt to fit the complex world into preconceived patterns (conceptual models or visions) of how things must be, and that this process leads to misunderstanding, misdescription and paradox. Philosophy is not a fact-finding activity – even though it thinks of itself in this way.

> Logic lay, it seemed, at the bottom of all of the sciences. For logical investigation explores the nature of all things. It seeks to see to the bottom of things and is not meant to concern itself whether what actually happens is this or that. It takes its rise, not from an interest in the facts of nature, nor from a need to grasp causal connections; but from an urge to understand the basis, or essence, of everything empirical. Not, however, as if to this end we had to hunt out new facts; it is, rather, of the essence of our investigation that we do not seek to learn anything new by it. We want to understand something that is already in plain view. For this is what we seem in some sense not to understand. (*Philosophical Investigations*, 89)

What is it that is in plain sight and yet we do not understand? Take the notion of time, for instance; a philosophical subject if there ever were one. What is in plain sight are references we make to time in our everyday activities. In those references we show our mastery of the notion. And yet when we come to reflect on the concept itself our grip suddenly becomes insecure. 'We have got on to slippery ice,' he writes, and 'just because of that, we are unable to walk. We want to walk; so we need *friction*. Back to the rough ground' (*Philosophical Investigations*, 107). In Chapters 14–16 of the *Confessions* Augustine soliloquizes about time, and finds himself 'on slippery ice.'

> What is time? Who can easily and briefly explain this? Who can comprehend this even in thought, so as to express it in a word? Yet what do we discuss more familiarly and knowingly in conversation than time? Surely we understand it when we talk about it, and also understand it when we hear others talk about it. What, then, is time? If no one asks me, I know; if I want to explain it to someone who does ask me, I do not know …
>
> We term ten days ago, let us say, a short time past, and ten days to come, a brief future time. But in what sense is something non-existent either long or short? The past no longer exists, and the future is not yet in being. Therefore we should not say 'it is long,' but we

should say of the past, 'it was long,' and of the future 'it will be long.' … That past time which was so long, was it long when it was already past, or before that, when it was still present? It could be long at the time when that existed which could be long. Once past, it did not exist, hence it could not be long, since it in no wise existed. … See how the present time, which alone we found worthy to be called long, is contracted to hardly the space of a single day … one hour itself goes on in fleeting moments; whatever part of it has flown away is past, whatever remains is future. If any point of time is conceived that can no longer be divided into even the most minute parts of a moment, that alone it is which may be called the present. It flies with such speed from the future into the past that it cannot be extended by even a trifling amount. For if it is extended, it is divided into past and future. The present has no space. Where then is the time that we may call long? Is it to come? We do not say of it that it is long, because it does not yet exist, so as to be long. We say that it will be long. When, therefore, will it be? Even then, if it will be to come, it will not be long, since that which will be long does not yet be. … Still, O Lord, we perceive intervals of time. We compare them to one another and say that some are longer and some shorter. But it is passing times that we measure, and we make these measurements in perceiving them. Therefore, as long as time is passing by, it can be perceived and measured, but when it has passed by, it cannot be measured since it does not exist.

Is there some fact or set of facts about the nature of time that Augustine, as an ordinary person, lacks? Wittgenstein would say 'no.' Augustine concedes that he is not at a loss when it comes to the use of temporal terms in his everyday life. It is when he theorizes about the nature of time that it seems incredibly puzzling to him. But why should this be so? Wittgenstein's diagnosis in the *Brown Book* (pp. 107–109) is that a philosopher like Augustine is importing a certain conception or 'picture' of time in trying to understand what it is. That 'picture' seems to be that time is a kind of river, flowing by a fixed observer ('as long as time is passing by, it can be perceived and measured' Augustine says). In the following passage, which I shall quote in its entirety, Wittgenstein gives a brilliant diagnosis of how the Augustinian conception leads to intellectual puzzlement. He writes:

'Where does the present go when it becomes past, and where is the past?' – Under what circumstances has this question an allurement for us? For under certain circumstances it hasn't, and we should wave it away as nonsense.

It is clear that this question most easily arises if we are preoccupied with cases in which there are things flowing by us, – as logs of wood float down a river. In such a case we can say the logs which have passed us are all down towards the left and the logs which will pass us are up towards the right. We then use this situation as a simile for all happening in time and even embody the simile in our language, as when we say that 'the present event passes by' (a log passes by), 'the future event is to come' (a log is to come). We talk about the flow of events; but also about the flow of time – the river on which the logs travel.

Here is one of the most fertile sources of philosophic puzzlement: we talk of the future event of something coming into my room and also of the future coming of this event.

We say, '*Something* will happen', and also, 'Something comes towards me'; we refer to the log as 'something', but also the log's coming towards me.

Thus it can come about that we aren't able to rid ourselves of the implications of our symbolism, which seems to admit of a question like 'Where does the flame of a candle go when it's blown out?', 'Where does the light go to?', 'Where does the past go to?' We have become obsessed with our symbolism – We may say that we are led into puzzlement by an analogy which irresistibly drags us on. – And this also happens when the meaning of the word 'now' appears to us in mysterious light. In our example 55) it appears that the function of 'now' is in no way comparable to the function of an expression like 'five o'clock', 'midday', 'the time when the sun sets', etc. This latter group of expressions I might call 'specifications of times'. But our ordinary language uses the word 'now' and specifications of times in similar contexts. Thus we say

'The sun sets at six o'clock'.
'The sun is setting now'.

We are inclined to say that both 'now' and 'six o'clock' 'refer to points of time'. This use of words produces a puzzlement which one might express in the question: 'What is the 'now'? – for it is a moment of time and yet it can't be said to be either 'the moment at which I speak' or 'the moment at which the clock strikes', etc., etc.' – Our answer is: The function of the word 'now' is entirely different from that of a specification of time – This can easily be seen if we look at the role this word really plays in our usage of language, but it is obscured when instead of looking at the *whole language game*, we only look at the contexts, the phrases of language in which the word is used. (The word 'today' is not a date, but it isn't anything like it either. It doesn't differ from a date as a hammer differs from a mallet, but as a hammer differs from a nail; and surely we may say there is both a connection between a hammer and a mallet and and between a hammer and a nail.)

One has been tempted to say that 'now' is the name of an instant of time, and this, of course, would be like saying that 'here' is the name of a place, 'this' the name of a thing, and 'I' the name of a man.

As Wittgenstein points out, this vision of time as a flowing river carries with it certain implications: just as the river is extended in space, so time, it would seem, is extended in space, having forward and backward parts. This 'picture' seems intuitively plausible and moreover to fit the facts, for it does seem as if time flows, moving as it were past a motionless percipient.

Yet for Augustine this picture gives rise to deep perplexities: if the past and future do not exist and the present – the so-called 'now' – has no space, then what has happened to the river of time? A river always remains extended, having parts that have not yet reached an observer, parts that an observer can now see, and parts that have passed the observer. We can speak of the reach of the river that has not yet arrived as being of a certain length and similarly of the part that has passed and is on its way to the sea. But if one holds that neither the past nor the future now exists, the river model of time does not help us explain what we ordinarily mean when we speak of the distant past or of a long prospective future. And even worse, if the present 'now' is instantaneously disappearing into the past and being replaced by an ever intruding future, at what time has the river passed our 'fixed observer'? And does 'fixed' mean that the observer is somehow not in time? But surely that is impossible. Yet what other conception of time might one have, except as something that flows? The picture seems unavoidable to the reflective person.

Wittgenstein generalizes from the case of Augustine. All power-ful philosophical insights will issue in pictures or conceptual models of this sort, models that are unremitting in their hold on the reflective individual. We say of the world 'this is how it has to be.' As Wittgenstein puts it, 'a picture held us captive. And we could not get outside of it, for it lay in our language and language seemed to repeat it to us inexorably.' These pictures force themselves upon us; they seem unavoidable and to be great philosophical discoveries. They help make sense of our ambience by illuminating it like flashlights that cast spears of light into the dark. Another example of such a model would be the notion that human beings are nothing but machines: the kind of model we find in Hobbes, who asks: 'What is the heart but a spring; what are the nerves but so many strings?' This is a picture that is today accepted by many eliminative materialists. Such a picture does provide an ordering scheme for comprehending the world. But just as Augustine's conception of time leads to paradox so does this conception. It does so by obliterating the differences between such things as computers and human beings, subsuming both under the category of machine. It is this obliteration of distinctions we make in every-day life – in 'the language game' – that is a mark of paradox; tradi-tional philosophy in its quest to order reality via some simple but powerful conceptual model will inevitably issue in paradox, i.e., in a constricted and distorted picture of the world. One cannot there-fore do philosophy in that way; some alternative to it is thus needed. But what could it be? This is what Wittgenstein's new method is designed to provide.

There is thus a second conception of philosophy referred to in Wittgenstein's later works, one designed to give us a better under-standing of the world than traditional philosophy and, in particular, one designed to avoid paradox. The two conceptions are contrasted in this passage:

> The real discovery is the one that makes me capable of stopping doing philosophy when I want to. The one that gives philosophy peace, so that it is no longer tormented by questions which bring itself in question.

The first occurrence of 'philosophy' in this passage refers to the traditional way of doing philosophy, one that issues in paradox and in self-torment. But, as the second occurrence indicates, this older way can be avoided or suppressed and can be replaced by a new way of doing philosophy – one that 'gives philosophy peace' – which Wittgenstein describes in a series of striking apothegms:

> The work of the philosopher consists in assembling reminders for a particular purpose. (127)

> Philosophy simply puts everything before us, and neither explains nor deduces anything. ... One might also give the name 'philosophy' to what is possible before all new discoveries and inventions. (126)

> We must do away with all explanation, and description alone must take its place. (109)

> If it is asked: 'How do sentences manage to represent?' – the answer might be: 'Don't you know? You certainly see it, when you use them.' For nothing is concealed. How do sentences do it? – Don't you know? For nothing is hidden. (435)

These comments about reminders, the hidden, and description are crucial to understanding the new way of doing philosophy. Wittgenstein agrees with the traditional philosopher that the facts are complex. Our ordinary ways of characterizing time are enormously complicated: these characterizations are embedded in a multiplicity of idioms in which the notion of time plays a role. The philosopher, looking carefully at this multifarious array of idioms, wishes to discover a comprehensible order in it, and does so by trying to look deeper – to find the essence or real meaning of time itself.

What Wittgenstein says in opposition to this highly intuitive philosophical move is: Don't do it! Do not attempt to look more deeply! Instead, he urges, look more closely at how these expressions are used in the language game – the *whole* language game. And then you will understand what time is – for nothing in the language game is hidden. He is stressing that your everyday practice reveals that you know what time is; that you have a mastery of the concept. This is, in part, what Wittgenstein means by saying that the purpose of descriptive philosophy is 'to leave everything as it is.' One who looks closely at how temporal expressions are employed in daily life will realize that this is what 'time' means. By describing such uses, he will not impose a factitious conceptual model on actual practice, but will 'leave everything as it is.' He will thus eventually 'see the world rightly.'

Augustine has admitted that he has no problems in everyday life in employing the notion of time. What he fails to understand is that his everyday employment of the concept is a mastery. And he also fails to understand that because that is so there are no residual problems about time to be solved. Thus, Wittgenstein emphasizes that Augustine's problems are of his own making. He wishes to impose a model that will simplify and order a seemingly chaotic set of uses of the concept of time. But this is both unnecessary and confusing. As Bishop Berkeley was later to say, 'We first cast up a dust and then complain we cannot see.'

So Wittgenstein's first step in developing an alternative philosophy to this older way is to say that no real facts about time are at issue. No facts are missing and there is nothing left to be explained. Virtually everyone knows how to use the concept in his or her daily life and so everyone knows what time is. What Wittgenstein is urging us to see is that there is no theoretically adequate description of time because 'time' is used in many ad hoc ways. What is true of the concept of time is true of all the concepts philosophers have traditionally analyzed: knowledge, truth, certainty, name, object, etc. It will be a function of the new philosophy to remind traditional philosophers that in every case they possess such knowledge. As he writes:

> When philosophers use a word – 'knowledge,' 'being,' 'object,' 'I,' 'proposition,' 'name' – and try to grasp the essence of the thing, one must always ask oneself: is the word ever actually used in this way in the language-game which is its original home?
> What we do is to bring words back from their metaphysical to their everyday use. (*Philosophical Investigations*, 116)

It is difficult to overestimate the originality and historical importance of Wittgenstein's assessment of traditional philosophy and the alternative he is proposing to it. In effect, he is standing the received view about the nature of philosophy on its head. Since the time of the Greeks the commonly accepted view draws a contrast between the philosopher and the ordinary person. It is the latter who is not reflective, who lives the unexamined life, who blindly follows conventions and authority (especially political authority), who lives in the world of appearance, to use Plato's phrase, and is cut off from reality. By contrast, it is the philosopher probing beneath the surface who discovers (or at least tries to discover) reality. It is the philosopher who exposes the shallowness of the everyday conventions we all follow and who, by such probing, discovers the true nature of things. Socrates is the model of the exemplary philosopher, ultimately condemned to death by plain men, terrified by his obsessive search for truth. That the philosopher holds the key to wisdom, knowledge and truth has been the accepted picture since time immemorial – accepted by nearly all intellectuals as well as by most common persons – and it is part and parcel of this view to denigrate the proverbial 'plain man.'

But Wittgenstein's originality consists in turning this picture on its head. It is the plain man who is all right, who is not troubled by mental cramps, and who does not cast up a dust that prevents him from seeing things as they are. It is rather the traditional philosopher who does these things, who cannot see what is in front of his face, and who in looking for the hidden is only chasing chimeras. In Wittgenstein we thus find the deepest challenge to the widely espoused picture of traditional philosophy. But that does not mean that Wittgenstein rejects philosophy entirely; instead he wishes to replace the older conception, with its vision of the invidious relationship between the philosopher and the ordinary person, with an entirely different one.

When he says: 'what we do is to bring words back,' the 'we' is referring to himself and to a new way of doing philosophy: a way that will give us an accurate picture of the world, i.e., of the features we encounter in everyday life. It will be non-distorting because it will flatly describe what is there 'on the surface.' It will not attempt to explain the world's surface features by looking for what lies beneath them, for such an explanation is at least redundant and at worst misleading. This careful description will thus function as a set of reminders of what each of us has always known, including those who do traditional philosophy. But unlike the ordinary person, traditional philosophers set aside what they have always known because they are in the grip of a powerful conceptual model. In their search for a deeper explanation (normally a theory) they suppress the facts (say about time) that are available to everyone. Nothing beyond those facts is needed to understand the temporal aspects of the world. To remind oneself of those facts is to 'leave everything as it is.' One who can do this will thus 'see the world rightly.'

I will say more below about Wittgenstein's new way of doing philosophy; but now let us turn to his use of the 'broken text' as a seminal element in the method that the new philosophy should employ.

The broken text

By 'broken text,' I mean a style of writing that is non-systematic, rambling, digressive, discontinuous, interrupted thematically and marked by rapid transitions from one subject to another. A broken text typically takes the form of pithy remarks, such as maxims, apothegms, aphorisms, short paragraphs or other sorts of scattered fragments. These short sayings function as the basic units by which the author wishes to communicate his thoughts. It is also generally characterized by a lack of explicit argumentation. One is moved conceptually and presumably will eventually come to possess a point of view one did not hold before; but it is not arrived at through tight argumentation. In that sense, the broken text is to be distinguished from more standard, discursive forms of writing in which ideas are coherently organized and disseminated in larger units: sections, chapters, or even whole books. One might briefly characterize any such broken text as a collection of snippets. No wonder that Wittgenstein called one of his bundles of notes, mostly composed between 1945–1948, *Zettel* (*Scraps*). This literary style has ancient antecedents, in Hippocrates and Heraclitus, for example; it is also found in such later authors as Leonardo, Bacon, Pascal, Vico, Kierkegaard, Nietzsche, Karl Kraus, Gramsci, Heidegger, N. O. Brown, Barthes, and Derrida; and as this list indicates, it can be used for both philosophical and non-philosophical purposes. Wittgenstein is, of course, the consummate master of this mode of writing in philosophy.

The use of the broken text is generally not accidental but purposive and it is commonly used in adversarial or even subversive ways. In such cases it is used to challenge standard or received ways of representing various features of the world, such as those expressed in the 'spare, pure, transparent language' of traditional philosophy. Wittgenstein's use of it is characteristic. He is reacting against any attempt by philosophers to understand the world in neat and sharp categories. His invocation of the method thus rests on a number of presuppositions: first, that the world is complex; second, that no simple conceptual model of the sort traditional philosophy imposes on those facts will accommodate their variety, and accordingly that all forms of reductionism will eventually fail; third, that a discursive, organized, argumentative literary style is part and parcel of reductionist model building; and fourth, that the new mode of doing philosophy, in which description replaces explanation, requires a different literary style. As he puts it succinctly in the Preface to the *Investigations*, his use of that style is 'connected with the very nature of the investigation. For this compels us to travel over a wide field of thought criss-cross in every direction.'

Three further comments should be made in discussing this topic. First, the frequent appearance of aphorisms and apothegms does not entail that a text is broken. Historically, there have been many documents replete with aphorisms, among them the *Tractatus*, that lack the characteristic features of broken texts. Even in works like the *Investigations* and *On Certainty*, in which aphorisms and a broken text are present, and closely intertwined, it is important that this discrimination be made. Second, the notion of the broken text should not itself be identified with any particular method, though once again in the case of Wittgenstein his method and the use of a broken text are intimately laced together. In this instance one might think of the broken text as a special device or technique used to enhance the effectiveness of a certain method. Third, Wittgenstein's method, using the technique of the broken text, is designed for certain specific purposes, mainly to break the hold which conceptual models exercise on philosophers. I will now speak briefly on each of these points.

As I mentioned above, Wittgenstein uses apothegms and aphorisms in the *Tractatus*, but it would be a mistake to infer from this practice that we are dealing with an exemplar of the broken text. The broken text, as defined above, is non-systematic, digressive and not marked by a tight logical structure. The text of the *Tractatus*, in contrast, exhibits just such features. It is highly organized, with major sections being defined by single natural numbers from 1 through 7. Subsections are organized in progressively narrowing numbers, according to topic and to the thrust of the argument. We thus have a schema which, say, starts with a major section, such as 3, moves to subordinate sections such as 3.01, 3.03, 3.031, 3.1432, and so on. As distinct from the use of aphorisms in the later writings, there is a coherent, tightly knit pattern of ratiocination in the *Tractatus*. The aphorism is used there as a summary of lengthy reflections engaged in elsewhere and not recorded in the text. Rather than trying to accommodate all the complexities that those reflections uncovered, Wittgenstein's method in the *Tractatus* was to extract an essential point from them and to incorporate it into a maxim (e.g., 'Roughly speaking, objects are colorless.'). As he was to say later (and in a different context) he was condensing a 'whole cloud of philosophy into a drop of grammar.' The effort to distill philosophical reflection into such a small compass is precisely the opposite technique exhibited by the diffuse ramification of apothegms in his later work.

Further, it is necessary to distinguish the broken text as a literary style from its philosophical purpose. A new philosophical method, such as Wittgenstein developed, is connected with its aim; what it hopes to achieve in the understanding or resolution of philosophical problems. It is thus possible for a philosopher to use the technique of the broken text but to use it for familiar or conventional philosophical purposes. We can illustrate the point with reference to Pascal's *Pensées*. Pascal's purpose in using a broken text was completely different from Wittgenstein's. His aim was to convert free thinkers (libertins) to Christianity. His literary style took the form of fragments, often aphoristic in nature, describing in multifarious idioms what is wrong with those whose lives are devoted to the pursuit of pleasure and the gratification of their egos, and whose intellectual stance is an agnosticism derived from Montaigne. But that technique was put to a well-known philosophical use: to defend a traditional religious point of view. The broken text of the *Pensées* was thus mustered not in the service of a special method for rethinking the nature of the problems its author wished to grapple with so much as to defend a familiar solution to them.

This brings us then to Wittgenstein's method per se; what he was trying to achieve by using the various literary devices he employs. As we have seen, Wittgenstein believes that traditional philosophers are gripped by pictures that 'bewitch the intelligence.' These pictures are designed to give human beings a deeper, more penetrating understanding of the world and certain of its features. But the application of these pictures gives rise to perplexity, puzzlement, and anomaly. These difficulties, he contends, are not empirical and therefore cannot be solved by an appeal to the facts. As he says: 'The problems are solved, not by giving new information, but by arranging what we have always known' (*Philosophical Investigations*, 109). The new method is devoted to helping philosophers rearrange what they have always known.

In one of his books, Wittgenstein gives an example of how a certain problem is solved by 'arranging what we have always known.' He says: suppose you have a bookcase whose books are arranged in a certain fashion – say, alphabetically by title. But the arrangement puts books of quite different sizes and heights cheek by jowl. The arrangement does not appeal to you. So you rearrange them according to height. Now they look OK. No new fact (book) has been introduced; it is the same collection you started with. But in their new grouping the collection somehow looks different and indeed better. The analogy explains what he thinks the purpose of philosophy is. By helping you rearrange what you have always known philosophy can help you see the world in a different way. In doing this it does not discover anything new about the world; but it makes you look at it differently. That is what his new method is designed to do. It changes your picture of things. I shall illustrate this point on page 100 with a detailed example.

I pointed out at the beginning of this chapter that Wittgenstein never explicitly describes what his method is and what it is supposed to achieve. One must put together a range of more or less exiguous hints in arriving at an interpretation of what he believes he is doing. With respect to what the method is supposed to accomplish, I submit that it is designed to do two things: first, to loosen or eliminate the grip that certain conceptual models exercise on philosophers, and second, to make explicit, via a set of reminders, the actual roles that various concepts play in our everyday lives.

With respect to the first point, we can say that the Wittgensteinian diagnosis of what is wrong with traditional philosophy resembles (as has been emphasized by John Wisdom) the diagnosis that a psychoanalyst might make of a neurotic patient. Let us say that the patient is suffering from a form of paranoia. He believes that someone (some unknown person) is trying to poison him. Suppose the analyst tries to explain to his client that there is no evidential basis for his belief. As the history of psychoanalysis makes abundantly clear, that approach would be unsuccessful. An appeal to the facts will not ultimately influence the patient; on the contrary he will absorb them into his model and thus neutralize their impact. The patient's problem is thus not resolvable by bringing more information to his attention. The analyst must instead somehow develop a method that will alter the patient's conceptual set. In effect, the analyst is trying to replace one (a misleading) world view with another (the view that the analyst represents, and that most normal persons hold). The latter is the 'correct' view; it is in opposition to the one that the patient holds. The change would consist in bringing the patient back to 'normality,' to possessing an outlook that will allow the facts to play their normal roles in his life.

There is a wonderful example in *On Certainty* that illustrates these points. I will quote the whole passage, which stresses that when differing conceptual models are in opposition an appeal to the facts will not typically resolve the conflict between them. Some rearrangement is required. Here is the passage:

> However, we can ask: May someone have telling grounds for believing that the earth has only existed for a short time, say since his own

birth? – Suppose he had always been told that, – would he have any good reason to doubt it? Men have believed that they could make rain; why should not a king be brought up in the belief that the world began with him? And if Moore and this king were to meet and discuss, could Moore really prove his belief to be the right one? I do not say that Moore could not convert the king to his view, but it would be a conversion of a special kind; the king would be brought to look at the world in a different way.

Remember that one is sometimes convinced of the correctness of a view by its simplicity or symmetry, i.e., these are what induce one to go over to this point of view. One then simply says something like: 'That's how it must be.' (*On Certainty*, 92)

When Wittgenstein says that if Moore could convert the king to his point of view it would be a conversion of a special kind, he is emphasizing that an appeal to the facts will not in general change one's deepest picture of the world; that picture is too firmly embedded for the facts to do their normal work. Some other way needs to be pursued to effect such a conversion.

I am not here asserting that Wittgenstein was intentionally aping the methods of psychoanalysis, but merely that there are striking similarities. But there is at least one important difference, and this is to be found in the second point I mentioned above. Wittgenstein wishes the philosopher to learn something by reading books like *Philosophical Investigations* or *On Certainty*. He does not merely wish to dissolve the hold that a certain picture exercises, but to give the philosopher an appreciation for a set of facts that person has overlooked or minimized. This will consist in a detailed and positive account of the roles played in 'the language game' (i.e., in everyday life) by certain important notions: knowledge, certainty, doubt, proof, evidence, and so forth. I take it that the psychoanalytic process does not issue in positive learning of this sort. Wittgenstein's main problem, which the methodology is dedicated to resolving, is how to bring about the kind of attitude in a philosopher which will allow him to learn positive things of this sort. In facing this kind of difficulty, he is confronting a problem not unlike that which the analyst faces and that is why he feels it important to weaken the hold that a picture exercises.

Unless one starts in this way the philosopher will be resistant to Wittgenstein's reminders. As we have seen, Augustine knows all the facts there are to know about time and yet remains puzzled. Therefore, he must somehow be maneuvered or manipulated into the position of giving up the model that time is a river. When that has been achieved, he can attain a state of mind in which he will recognize and acknowledge his actual command of the ordinary temporal idioms. But before one can cross that bridge there is a first step to take: how can one get a philosopher to abandon a picture whose hold seems inexorable? Wittgenstein's method is designed to meet that challenge.

In explaining this first step, this first element in Wittgenstein's method, one finds the psychoanalytic analogy helpful to some extent. The basic technique of Freudian analysis is the method of free associ-ation. The patient's associations, embedded in talk, gradually reveal to the analyst where a particular model is exercising its grip. But more important, of course, those associations freely expressed will begin to reveal this to the patient himself. That person will eventually come to understand that his neurosis is based upon an incorrect assessment of certain aspects of reality; that his behavior and attitudes are driven by a false picture. In those cases where a cure is effected the patient will come to an assessment of his situation in the way that any non-neurotic person would. He will then be free of an incubus, of the picture that held him captive. A philosopher reading the later Wittgenstein will find in the broken text something like free associa-tion. That play of aphorisms, apparently unstructured, will do for the philosopher who is willing to tolerate this 'criss-cross' movement of ideas something comparable to what free association will do for the neurotic patient. It should liberate him from the conceptual set in which he is embedded and which forces a certain way of looking at the world upon him.

I said that something like free association is going on here. But we must not exaggerate the psychoanalytic analogy. Wittgenstein is not a psychoanalyst. There is no particular patient he is trying to treat, and there is no one in his 'office' who is freely associating. Nor is Wittgenstein freely associating in his notebooks. He may not know in advance what the best formulation of a point is; but his approach is not random. He has a definite purpose in mind. Rather than freely associating, he is in control.

Examples and cases

The aphoristic style Wittgenstein uses in the *Investigations* has one further and important advantage. It allows him to depict features of the language game more easily than a discursive, argumentative style would. All of his later philosophy is replete with detailed examples, including what he calls *zwischengliedern* (intermediate cases). The point of this welter of examples, analogies, metaphors and cases is to induce the reader to see that no general theory will accommodate the complexity of the real world.

The method of cases often relies on appeals to ordinary language, but such appeals should be distinguished from the method itself. For example, the language games that begin the *Investigations* describe a number of different situations (cases) involving a pair of builders, but the points Wittgenstein wishes to make in describing those situations do not depend on distinctions drawn from ordinary language. However, let's look at an example which exhibits Wittgenstein's typical use of the method in which infusions from ordinary language do play important roles:

> Compare *knowing* and *saying*:
> how many feet high Mont Blanc is –
> how the word 'game' is used –
> how a clarinet sounds

> If you are surprised that one can know something and not be able to say it, you are perhaps thinking of a case like the first. Certainly not of one like the third. (*Philosophical Investigations*, 78)

In this passage Wittgenstein is describing the difference in everyday use between the concepts of knowing and saying. If Augustine had 'looked more closely' at the temporal idioms used in ordinary discourse his puzzles about time might never have arisen. In the above example, Wittgenstein is doing two things: he is first of all depicting a difference in use between such concepts as knowing and saying, but he is also calling attention to a conceptual model that tends illicitly to assimilate these to one another. He is urging the reader to see for himself that a model that applies to the question 'How many feet high is Mont Blanc?' does not apply to the question 'How does a clarinet sound?' His point is that it is not surprising if a person were to state that he knows how a clarinet sounds but can't say how it sounds; but that it would be surprising if that person were to aver that he knows how high Mont Blanc is but can't say how high it is. It is part of everyday living to expect that if someone knows the height of something he should be able to say what it is; hence, the surprise if this relationship fails. In contrast, many persons know how a clarinet sounds but practically nobody can say what the sound is. We simply do not have the vocabulary to do so. Therefore, the contrast between knowing and saying is not surprising in this case.

By means of this example, Wittgenstein is saying something that every ordinary person would agree with. He is doing philosophy in the new way. He is using the example to *remind* persons of things they in fact know; but strangely enough are unaware that they know. This is because, as he writes, they are 'captured by a picture,' i.e., a conceptual model which impels them to think that if you know something you should *in every case* be able to say what it is that you know. The model does work for a restricted range of cases. If I know how far it is from Los Angeles to San Francisco I can say what the distance is. But the model has a limited application. It does not apply to all cases where knowing and saying are compared and contrasted. And that is what his descriptive method is designed to bring out. It distinguishes between cases. The case of Mont Blanc and of the clarinet are different in important respects. But that is just the way life is. There is no one theory or general philosophical account that will fit the whole range of different situations, cases, and activities we find in everyday existence. So a new method of doing philosophy is needed to bring out just how complex the world is. Wittgenstein's technique does not depend on any theory. He is rejecting what he calls 'an explanation.' He is just describing the facts. But these descriptions are more than merely 'semantic' in their import. They are descriptions of everyday life.

They are reminders for his readers of what ordinary, everyday life is like. And in that sense they are informative. We have learned something by 'looking more closely' at our ongoing activities. But in doing so, we have not changed anything in our lives; instead, we have left 'everything as it is.' And this is the positive outcome of his new method.

The use of the broken text in Wittgenstein's later writings is intimately connected with the method of cases. It allows him great flexibility in describing and then discussing a wide variety of cases, without being tied to a conventional organizational schema. It is the perfect literary mechanism for the use of the criss-cross technique. And in aphorism after aphorism, building upon example piled upon example, it allows the method to have its maximum effect.

The point of the method should now be apparent. It is designed to sensitize the philosopher to the complex ways in which various cases resemble and differ from one another. The message Wittgenstein wishes to communicate is that how we speak about, understand, and assess various features of the world and its inhabitants will depend on the subtle discriminations we make between resembling and yet differing cases. The philosophical significance of the method is that no overarching, synoptic theory or conceptual model will do justice to this variety of cases. The import of this method is thus two-fold: to assist the philosopher in freeing himself from the compulsion to make such generalizations; and secondly to make him realize that there is much to be learned about the world and its diverse features by comparing and discriminating these cases from one another.

Language games

A third feature of the new method is its description and use of what Wittgenstein calls 'language games.' This concept was first expounded in the *Brown Book* of 1934. This is a work that he himself did not write but dictated to two of his students, Francis Skinner and Alice Ambrose. People who borrowed these notes made their own copies, and, as Rush Rhees states, 'there was a trade in them.' The *Blue Book* was based on lectures he had given a year earlier. The *Brown Book* contains seventy-three 'language games.' Each is said to be fully complete in itself and each describes a possible situation, for example in which a builder is speaking to an assistant. The concept of a language game became one of the key devices of the later philosophy and is found extensively in such works as *Philosophical Investigations* and *On Certainty*. Curiously enough, a 'language game' is neither simply a game nor simply a use of certain linguistic expressions, though both of these features are frequently present in language games. Rather, a language game is a slice of everyday human activity; each slice is different; some may include the activities of builders, others of lawyers, and some may focus on such practices as affirming, doubting, believing, and following rules. Language games not only refer to individual human activities but to those that are common to the whole community. Their scope thus also comprises the happenings in such institutions as governments, universities, banks, the military, and so forth.

By appealing to language games, Wittgenstein is urging the traditional philosopher not to think but to look and see what persons actually do and say in the course of their daily lives. The description of such activities and utterances rather than a synoptic philosophical theory about them will provide an accurate picture of reality. Both the *Brown Book* and *Philosophical Investigations* open with a quotation from Augustine's *Confessions*. Augustine is giving an account of how children learn language. He says: 'When they (my elders) named some object and accordingly moved towards something, I saw this and I grasped that the thing was called by the sound they uttered when they meant to point it out.' Wittgenstein says that Augustine is trying to present 'a particular picture of the essence of human language. It is this: the individual words in language name objects – sentences are combinations of such names. ... In this picture of language we find the roots of the following idea: Every word has a meaning. This meaning is correlated with the word. It is the object for which the word stands' (*Philosophical Investigations*, 1). Augustine's picture of language is also Russell's in *Logical Atomism*, and Wittgenstein's in the *Tractatus*. Recall *Tractatus* 3.203, 'The name means the object. The object is its meaning.'

Wittgenstein's point here is not that this picture is absolutely wrong, but rather that it is a restricted picture of how language functions in real life. As the collection of language games builds up in *Philosophical Investigations*, one can see that language has many other uses. This is what Wittgenstein means when he says that a picture held us captive and when he advises philosophers not to think but to look closely. To urge philosophers to look is to ask them to expand their conceptual categories, to see how words function in the stream of life. As Wittgenstein puts it in a brilliant metaphor:

> Think of the tools in a tool-box; there is a hammer, pliers, a saw, a screwdriver, a rule, a glue-pot, glue, nails and screws. The functions of words are as diverse as the functions of these objects. (*Philosophical Investigations*, 11)

By producing a vast array of differing language games, Wittgenstein is reminding theorists that they are also ordinary human beings who use language according to the rules of the community they are reared in. The parade of language games will induce them to recall how in daily life they use such concepts as believing, doubting, proving, and justifying. These reminders call to their attention something they would recognize as correct if they reflected on what they say. Wittgenstein is thus helping them to attain this kind of self-awareness. This is different from what any philosopher has attempted to do. Consider knowing, for example. Wittgenstein produces dozens of examples in which 'I know' is used in ordinary discourse. These can be contrasted with the philosopher's use. G. E. Moore, for instance, claimed to know with certainty such propositions as 'The earth is very old,' or 'Other persons have existed and many now exist.' He also claimed that he knew that virtually every adult also knew these propositions to be true. Moore differs from Wittgenstein. He is not reminding persons of things they have always known but are not conscious of. He is telling them things that they are already fully aware of; so reminders are otiose. According to Wittgenstein, Moore's procedure is without grip. In linguistic terms it involves a misuse of 'I know.'

Suppose you are asked, 'Are you sure that Smith was really there for the opening?' and you respond by saying 'I know he was.' In that case, your intention is to give the interrogator information he did not previously possess. Had he possessed that information he would not have asked the question. Generally speaking, the use of 'I know' is *pointless* when you mention things that you know that everyone knows. Moore's use of it to inform others of what he knows they already know is thus a special kind of nonsense. This is the point Wittgenstein is making when he writes: 'But Moore chooses precisely a case in which we all seem to know the same as he … (*On Certainty*, 84). Or again, 'The truths which Moore says he knows are such as, roughly speaking, all of us know, if he knows them' (*On Certainty*, 100). 'Thus, it seems to me that I have known something the whole time and yet there is no meaning in saying so, in uttering this truth' (*On Certainty*, 466). Moore has imposed a conceptual model on the language game that distorts its nature. Such impositions of models are characteristic of traditional philosophizing. They should be replaced by looking closely at actual specimens of communication.

In the published materials we now have, Wittgenstein's writings range over a vast assortment of subjects, from the foundations of mathematics to discussions of Freud, Frazer, Mahler, Mendelssohn, the human mind, psychology, ethics, aesthetics, and the nature of color. Many of his comments are narrowly directed, e.g., to misuses and proper uses of the concept of justification, for example. It is thus impossible to describe in a limited space all the topics he examined and his various approaches to them. But in his most important later works, *Philosophical Investigations* and *On Certainty*, he has two targets in mind: Platonism and Cartesianism. It is clear that he regards these as central themes in the history of Western philosophy. From his perspective they provide virtually irresistible conceptual models, and indeed in certain ways overlap and intertwine. Nearly all the major problems of traditional philosophy – change, universals, abstract ideas, skepticism, meaning, reference, and mind – derive from the thought of Plato and Descartes. We shall conclude this discussion with a brief account of his objections to their views. We shall find that misconceptions of how language functions play essential roles in their conceptual schemes.

Platonism

In order to explain Wittgenstein's treatment of Platonism we have first to understand Plato's theory of knowledge, and to understand that we must make a brief excursion into the historical background that Plato inherited. As I mentioned earlier, the ancient Greeks were obsessively speculative thinkers. Perhaps the most challenging problem they addressed was: 'What is the world really like?' Or in an alternative formulation, they sometimes put the question this way: 'Is the world made of some fundamental stuff, and if so, what is it?'

Two incompatible answers were given to these questions. One of them, advanced by Heraclitus (540?–475 B.C.) was that there was no fundamental stuff, i.e., nothing that was wholly immune to change. For him the only reality was the process of change itself. Everything is in flux, so that, as he remarks, 'You cannot step into the same river twice.' Every feature of the world comes into being and passes away. The only thing that does not change is a cosmic balance maintained by the continuous alteration of everything. There is no underlying 'stuff,' like water, as Thales believed, that remains invariant through all temporal processes. Though he himself apparently did not draw explicit skeptical implications from this view, some of his followers did. One of them, Cratylus (after whom Plato named a dialogue), held that reality is unintelligible. Since it does not stand still long enough to be described, our words and their meanings are constantly changing, as is each speaker. Thus human language is simply gibberish, having no fixed meanings; and accordingly discourse about the world is impossible. The Cratylean idea that change affects meaning was important for Plato, and then, as we shall see, for Wittgenstein as well.

An opposite point of view was espoused by Parmenides. His theory starts from the common sense observation that if something, say a leaf, changes, then to speak of it as a 'leaf' is to imply that some essential feature of it remains constant. Change is thus different from a sequence of different appearances. If change were total, there would be no cohesive thing that changed. In that case, a so-called 'leaf' would consist of a number of unconnected states that appear successively in one's visual field. Thus, a leaf must, as a matter of logic, have an essence, i.e., some 'stuff' that remains constant, and this, as distinct from its color, size, and shape, cannot be anything accessible to the senses. The Parmenidean thesis that the immutability of the world entails the existence of essences influenced both Plato and Wittgenstein, but in entirely different ways.

Given this intuition, Parmenides produced a set of arguments to show that reality is unchanging and cannot be accessed via sense experience. His name for reality is 'Being.' Being is the fundamental stuff of which the world is made. It cannot come into existence or pass away and that means it is permanent. Parmenides invented a series of clever arguments in support of this position. Suppose one believes that Being must have come from something. If true, that belief would imply that there was a time at which Being did not exist. But then what could it have come from? It could not come from itself, so it must have come from something other than Being. But anything other than Being is Non-Being, and by definition Non-Being does not exist. Accordingly, Non-Being (the Non-Existent) cannot produce anything, since it is nothing. Therefore, Being cannot come into existence at all, and this means that it has always existed. Another version of the argument proves that Being is a single fundamental stuff. Suppose one assumes that Being is composed of parts. Then these parts would be either real or not real. If they are not real, they do not exist and cannot be part of anything, let alone Being. If they are real, then they are not different from Being. Being is therefore one indissoluble stuff. By a similar argument Parmenides concluded that Being cannot move. To move to a place means to move to something that either exists or does not exist. But nothing can move to what does not exist, since it is not a place. Therefore, every existing place is occupied by Being. It follows that Being cannot move at all, and therefore that it cannot pass away. So it cannot cease to exist. Accordingly, these arguments show that Being is neither created nor destroyed, namely that it is unchanging and permanent.

The outcome of this train of reasoning was the rejection of the information derived from sense experience. According to the senses, things are seen, felt, and heard to shift position. But as the Parmenidean arguments show, reality cannot move; therefore motion is illusory. Since knowledge must be of that which is real, then if we are to have knowledge, it cannot be derived from sense experience. His view is thus a radical form of rationalism.

Plato's theory of knowledge is a tilted compromise between these two positions. It agrees with Heraclitus that sense experience reveals only change and nothing permanent. But it tilts toward the Parmenidean theses that one cannot know that which is in flux and that there exists an unchanging, knowable reality. It also concurs that to access the real world one must transcend sense experience. But it denies that the objects revealed by the senses are *wholly* unreal. Sense experience gives us some information but it falls short of knowledge. It thus rejects the Parmenidean notion that motion is entirely illusory. What is being affirmed instead is that perception can never result in knowledge. On the whole, then, the Platonic view emphasizes the role of reason, while it does not totally denigrate sense experience.

Let us now briefly examine what Plato says about sense experience. In Book VII of *The Republic*, in 'The Doctrine of the Divided Line,' we find an extensive treatment of this topic. In that passage, Plato distinguishes between the World of Appearance and the World of Reality. The World of Appearance is the world revealed to the senses. It consists of different sorts of objects. Each type of object is apprehended by a different mode of sensing. There are images, for instance, captured by the imagination; there are visible objects, such as tables and rocks, which are apprehended by sight and touch. Plato suggests that these objects can be arrayed in a spectrum of increasing stability. Images are more fleeting than rocks, for example. So the information we acquire about rocks is better than that about transient images. But such information never reaches certitude. For that we must access unchanging objects in the World of Reality. These he calls 'forms' or 'ideas' and we shall speak about them in a moment.

Plato says two things about sense experience that explain why it cannot produce knowledge. First, he states that the various objects one apprehends through the senses bear incompatible predicates. Thus, the same rock can be said to be light or heavy. Second, he points out that all such objects are subject to ceaseless change, though of course, some alter more rapidly than others. Therefore, because these objects change and have incompatible features, they *cannot be known*. Though he does not expand on these arguments, he seems to be suggesting that knowing is a kind of intellectual grasping. If an object changes, then one cannot really grasp it; it is like trying to pick up quicksilver. Moreover, if it has incompatible features, it has no consistent, and therefore no real, nature. It is merely a collection of appearances. Therefore, to acquire knowledge, one must leave the world of appearance and access those eternal and self-consistent objects that belong to the world of reality.

This view runs directly counter to any form of skepticism. Many forms of skepticism depend on showing that sense experience is fallible, and therefore that knowledge is impossible. Plato agrees with the skeptic that sense experience is corrigible, but denies that knowledge is impossible. His point is that in order to acquire knowledge one must leave the world of appearance, and in its place use reason. Plato's theory thus undercuts skepticism by co-opting one of its main principles, namely the unreliability of the senses, while attempting to show that the truth of this principle does not entail that knowledge is impossible. So how does Plato show that the use of reason will lead to the acquisition of knowledge? We turn to this complicated issue now: to his theory of forms.

Like the World of Appearance, the World of Reality is divided into objects and the capacities (Plato's word is 'faculties') humans can exercise to apprehend such objects. Plato also discriminates between lower and higher objects. The lowest of these are mathematical objects, such as numbers. Above them are the forms or ideas, and finally at the highest level there is one form which he calls *The Good*. There are then three levels of human faculties, each of which can be used to access these different types of objects. The lowest faculty is *thinking*, above it is *dialectic*, and still higher there is *intuition*, which can grasp The Good. The important points to remember about these objects are that they never change and that they are apprehensible only by the use of reason. In such works as *The Republic*, *Phaedo*, and *Timaeus*, Plato offers a plethora of arguments in defense of these theses. Given space limitations, it is impossible to reproduce any one of these arguments here in its actual detail. I will construct a simpler version of one such argument. Let us begin with the lowest sort of objects, numbers.

Suppose one were to write the following three inscriptions on a blackboard:

I, 1, –.

Each of these is a way of writing the number one (the first two belong to English, the third to Japanese). Now, as Plato says, reality cannot bear inconsistent predicates. That is why a rock, which can be light or heavy, cannot be real. Yet, the inscriptions we have just written do bear incompatible predicates. The second of these is to the left of '–' and to the right of 'I'. So it seems that numbers cannot belong to the World of Reality after all. But, wait, Plato would say. Suppose one were to erase the Japanese inscription. Would that mean that the number one no longer exists? Of course not. Suppose we erased all of these inscriptions; would that entail that the number one had been eliminated? Surely not! What Plato would say, and here he is supported by common sense, is that none of those inscriptions is the number one. Each is a symbolic *representation* of that number. Any attempt to write down or draw the number one will simply be a representation of it. It follows that there is no way of introducing the number one *itself* into the world of appearance. One can only produce representations of it. It follows that the number one does not exist in space or time at all. It cannot be written down, drawn, or pictured. If not, it cannot be erased either. Therefore, it cannot be brought into existence or be caused not to exist. This means that it is permanent. So there are objects, numbers being an example, that exist and yet do not change. Plato calls a sub-set of such objects 'forms' or 'ideas,' and asserts that they are constituents of the World of Reality. They are apprehended by a rational process called 'Dialectic.' This is a method of question and answer, designed to arrive at a so-called 'real definition.' A real definition will uncover the true meaning of a concept. Thus, the real definition of 'brother' is 'male sibling.' This process was invented and used by Socrates in questioning Athenians about the meaning of various terms, such as 'justice,' and 'piety.'

By 'idea' Plato does not mean anything psychological, such as my idea that it is now raining in San Diego. Ideas or forms are objective features of the world whose existence does not depend on their being thought of or perceived. The fact that they do not change and are internally consistent means that their existence in no way depends on human psychology. To understand what Plato means by 'forms' or 'ideas' we must note another distinction he draws, between particulars and non-particulars.

The idiograms we presented above of the number one each occupied a specific place in the space-time order. For example, 'I' was closer to the left edge of a page of this book than '1' was, and so forth. Anything that exists in the world of appearance can be localized in that way. This rock is exactly at this point in the garden, that chair is at a specific place in this room, and so forth. There was a time when the chair did not exist and there will be a time in the future when it does not exist. Its temporal career is thus localizable in much the same way that its spatial position is. Anything thus localizable in space and time is what Plato calls a *particular*. The theory of forms states that there are entities that are not so localizable. So a main characteristic of the forms is that they are non-particulars. Later, in the medieval period, they will be called 'universals.' Because they are not localizable, they do not exist in space and time. Since they are not exposed to the ravages of time, that means they are eternal. These are then the objects one must apprehend in order to acquire knowledge. Because they do not exist in space or time they cannot be seen, touched, tasted or heard. To apprehend them one must go beyond sense experience, and this consists in the use of reason.

What could such entities be? The explanation is difficult, but a common way of approaching the matter is by noting certain features of everyday language. Let us begin by distinguishing proper names from common names. Thus, I can use the proper name 'Citation' to *mean* a specific horse. That name picks out a specific animal, existing in a particular time and place. The author of the *Tractatus* would have said that the actual animal, Citation, is the *meaning* of the word 'Citation.' But then what does the term 'horse' refer to or pick out? Clearly it picks out anything that is a horse,

Citation, Secretariat, Seabiscuit, and so on. But it is not a proper name in the way that 'Citation' is. It does not pick out a particular horse. So it must mean something other than any particular horse. What it seems to mean is that feature or set of features that is essential to anything's being a horse. But what is that feature? It is not being a specific color or specific height or weight, because horses generally differ in such respects from one another. Let us call this feature a 'common element' or 'essence.' We can also say that it is the meaning of the word 'horse.'

Such general terms as *horse, brown, good, being to the right of* are ineliminable elements of our language. If we did not employ such terms it would be impossible to communicate or express any beliefs or thoughts. Any such thought will embed one of these general terms. But now observe that though we can point to Citation, we cannot in the same way point to *horse*. Anything we point to will be a specific horse. In Plato's parlance, it will be an example, representation, or instance of a horse, i.e., a 'particular.' Yet there must be something we mean when we use this term, and it cannot be a particular. It must thus be something that is non-particular. It is this meaning or essence that Plato is referring to when he speaks of 'forms' or 'ideas.'

We can now see the deep intuition that motivates Plato's theory of forms. First, he recognizes that in order to have knowledge one must use propositional language, i.e., form declarative sentences such as 'Citation is a horse.' In doing so, one is doing more than pointing to Citation. Pointing by itself does not give knowledge; one must go beyond pointing to speak assertorically and this requires a reference to the forms, i.e., to a common feature that all horses share in order to be a horse at all. Moreover, this feature is not itself something that exists in space and time. That is why we cannot see, point to, scratch or wash it. Even if Citation were to die, the form *horse* would still exist. If no horses were now alive, then *horse* would not be exemplified or represented in space and time. But that would not mean it would not exist. If all symbolic representations of the number one were to disappear, the number one would still exist. Forms are thus those entities denoted by common nouns and adjectives, words like 'red,' 'horse,' 'beauty,' and so forth.

Second, such essences are non-particular objects. As with a proper name, whose meaning is a particular object, the meaning of any common name is an object, but a non-particular one. Plato's theory thus thinks of meanings as objects. On such a view, to understand the meaning of a word is to grasp a particular kind of object. One of Wittgenstein's main objections to Platonism turns on this point. His view is that instead of thinking of meanings as objects we should emphasize the use that certain terms have in the language-game. To speak of 'use' in this way is to talk about the purposes to which language is being put. This new view of Wittgenstein's thus not only rejects Platonism but his own, earlier view in the *Tractatus*. Plato's theory of knowledge not only represents a compromise between the world of flux described by Heraclitus and the eternal, immobile world depicted by Parmenides, but it does so on the basis of a particular theory of meaning. That theory maintains that meanings (essences) are different from the symbols that humans use in everyday language. This is why in order to understand any statement one must go deeper than surface language to a world of hidden objects. This for Plato is a special function that the philosopher alone can exercise.

Wittgenstein begins his analysis of this model via its double conception of meaning as essence and meaning as an object underlying various linguistic expressions. The *Blue Book*, for instance, begins with the question, 'What is the meaning of a word?' The *Brown Book* and the *Investigations*, as I previously mentioned, begin with a discussion of a view about meaning that Augustine holds. What Wittgenstein shows in a brilliant, extended analysis is that the Platonic conception breaks down in a variety of ways. It fails, for example, to comprehend that one who knows the meaning of a common noun or adjective is not grasping an abstract entity but is able to use the word in various contexts for particular purposes. Instead of the Platonic model, with its emphasis upon the differing kinds of *objects* that words denote, Wittgenstein points out that the same linguistic expression may have a diversity of *uses*. In a striking metaphor he writes:

> Our language can be seen as an ancient city: a maze of little streets
> and squares, of old and new houses, and of houses with additions

> from various periods; and this surrounded by a multitude of new
> boroughs with straight regular streets and uniform houses.
> (*Philosophical Investigations*, 18)

The word 'game,' for instance, applies to many different kinds of
activities: some have explicit rules, such as chess; some involve
winning, some do not; some may be played by oneself, such as
throwing a ball against a wall. Therefore, to be a game is not necessarily to possess a feature it shares with all other games. For
Wittgenstein, the diversity of such linguistic uses reflects the diversity of the real world. Here in a famous passage is what he writes
about the many uses to which language is put:

> But how many kinds of sentence are there? Say assertion, question,
> and command? – There are countless kinds: countless different kinds
> of use of what we call 'symbols', 'words', 'sentences'. And this multi-
> plicity is not something fixed, given once for all; but new types of
> language, new language-games, as we may say, come into existence,
> and others become obsolete and get forgotten. (We can get a rough
> picture of this from the changes in mathematics.)
>
> Here the term 'language-game' is meant to bring into prominence
> the fact that the speaking of language is part of an activity, or a form
> of life.
>
> Review the multiplicity of language-games in the following exam-
> ples, and in others:
> Giving orders, and obeying them –
> Describing the appearance of an object, or giving its measurements –
> Constructing an object from a description (a drawing) –
> Reporting an event –
> Speculating about an event –
> Forming and testing a hypothesis –
> Presenting the result of an experiment in tables and diagrams –
> Making up a story; and reading it –
> Play-acting –
> Singing catches –
> Guessing riddles –
> Making a joke; telling it –
> Solving a problem in practical arithmetic –
> Translating from one language into another –
> Asking, thanking, cursing, greeting, praying –

It is interesting to compare the multiplicity of the tools in language and of the ways they are used, the multiplicity of the kinds of words and sentence, with what logicians have said about the structure of language. (Including the author of the *Tractatus Logico-Philosophicus.*) (*Philosophical Investigations*, 23)

In place of the Platonic view about essences, Wittgenstein suggests a new way of depicting how common nouns and adjectives work in everyday discourse. His name for this conception is 'family resemblance.' Consider how the members of a family resemble one another in certain ways and yet differ in certain ways. There is no essence they all share; but there are heaps of overlapping features. Think of their hair color. A and B may be blond, and blondness may take many forms. C and D, other members of the family, may not be blond, yet the texture and thickness of their hair may resemble those of A and B, and so forth. As Wittgenstein says:

I can think of no better expression to characterize these similarities than 'family resemblances'; for the various resemblances between members of a family: build, features, colour of eyes, gait, temperament, etc. etc. overlap and criss-cross in the same way. – And I shall say: 'games' form a family.

And for instance the kinds of number form a family in the same way. Why do we call something a 'number'? Well, perhaps because it has a – direct – relationship with several things that have hitherto been called number; and this can be said to give it an indirect relationship to other things we call the same name. And we extend our concept of number as in spinning a thread we twist fibre on fibre. And the strength of the thread does not reside in the fact that some one fibre runs through its whole length, but in the overlapping of many fibres.

But if someone wishes to say: 'There is something common to all these constructions – namely the disjunction of all their common properties' – I should reply: Now you are only playing with words. One might as well say: 'Something runs through the whole thread – namely the continuous overlapping of those fibres.' (*Philosophical Investigations*, 67)

Note his reference to the concept of number, and how it differs from Plato's view. There is no single 'fibre' that runs through all uses of this notion; instead the concept is a 'thread … [consisting of] the overlapping of many fibres.' The notion of 'family resemblance' is thus a descriptive term. It describes how concepts are actually employed in daily life. As such it is an antidote to the Platonic view about essences and objects. In this conception we see the method of cases at work. Wittgenstein is urging that one compare and contrast cases in order to see how words like 'number,' 'game,' and 'tool' are used in ordinary life. The method is applicable to all the concepts traditional philosophers have explored. It replaces the search for the essence of things and the need to 'penetrate phenomena' by an example-oriented, case by case description of the uses of words. This is how one arrives at a true understanding of reality.

Cartesianism

The other target of Wittgenstein's new method is the Cartesian model, which turns critically on an inner-outer distinction, involving a two-substance theory of reality. Mind and matter are two substances. Mind is an immaterial substance, lacking extension, mass, and locus. Matter is just the opposite: It has extension (length), bulk, and every material object has a specific location. According to Descartes, the distinction is both exhaustive and exclusive. In saying this, he means that everything that exists is either matter or mind, and that nothing is both. They are thus completely distinct from one another. As with all two-substance models, the Cartesian vision generates a problem about how the two substances can interact if they are so different. In this respect it is similar to Plato's quandary about how particulars can participate in the forms, since the former are in space and time and the latter are not. The Cartesian model raises a host of similar difficulties, for example how mental substance, which is immaterial, can interact with physical substance, which has mass and weight. How can something immaterial (mind) affect or cause something material (like an arm) to move when one decides to pick up a book? The model gives rise to two of the most forbidding perplexities in the philosophical lexicon: the External World and Other Minds problems. They are direct consequences of the model because the model identifies the mental with what is inner, the inner with what is private (with what is directly accessible to one only, i.e., to the proprietor of a particular mind), and the private with that which is hidden from others. The model thus suggests that each human being is encapsulated within the circle of his or her own ideas.

The difficulty is then how to emerge from this 'egocentric predicament.' According to the model, one has direct access to his or her own ideas, feelings and sensations, but no direct access to anything external, i.e., to the material world or to the minds of others. Such access, if possible at all, is at best inferential and at most probable. In one's own case certainty about one's ideas and feelings is possible because no inference is required. But this is a very restricted kind of certainty. It is limited to one's own sensations. So two perplexities immediately arise. First, the external world problem. It can be stated as follows: If the only evidence one has for anything are one's own subjective ideas, feelings, and sensations, what reason does anyone have to suppose that there is a reality external to those ideas and sensations? And even if there is such a reality, what reason does one have for supposing that one has accurate information (knowledge) about it? Second, there is the Other Minds difficulty. Since the internal sensations of others are hidden from any observer how can we ever know what another is thinking or whether another is in pain? In both cases, the threats of solipsism and skepticism are immediately entailed by the Cartesian conception.

Wittgenstein was obsessed with these two problems, and much of his later philosophy is devoted to analysing their sources in the Cartesian model and then showing how they can be neutralized. Because of the complexities both problems engender, we shall restrict our comments to one of them: the External World conundrum. In *Philosophical Investigations* and in *On Certainty* (written some fifteen years apart) Wittgenstein offers two radically different ways of resolving this problem. Both solutions are inventive and original. We shall speak about his views in *On Certainty* in the next chapter.

In the *Investigations* his discussion is ingenious; there is nothing like it in the previous literature. In effect, he argues that the

Cartesian model can be reinterpreted in a linguistic form. As such it gives rise to the notion of a wholly private language. Such a 'language' would be analogous to the 'egocentric predicament' that the Cartesian picture engenders. This is a language which presumably only one person could understand. That person would employ words in a singular way. Each word would stand for a particular object and only the user of the language would understand which object a particular word meant. (Compare such a model with Augustine's limited conception of the essence of language, or with Wittgenstein's in the *Tractatus*.) He would thus be using a system of private rules for designating the references of his words.

Nearly half of Part I of the *Investigations* (especially the segment 143–250) is dedicated to showing that no such conception of language is possible. For something to be a language it must be rule-governed. A linguistic rule is a piece of instruction about how various elements of the language are to be used. Wittgenstein points out that such rules must satisfy certain criteria: it must be possible to follow or violate a rule; rules are standards of correctness or guides to action; rules must be more or less transparent to participants in a rule-governed practice such as a language; the existence of rules presupposes their use in a human community; and finally the meanings of the words in a rule-governed language are independent of any particular person. This last criterion is critical. Its point is that each of us inherits a language. We inherit the rules for the standard use or uses of words, and we learn how to use such rules and the linguistic expressions they govern. So a language is something objective, not something subjective as the Cartesian outlook would imply. The late, distinguished American philosopher Norman Malcolm has given the clearest and most succinct interpretation of Wittgenstein's point of view about why a private language is not possible. He states:

> To speak a language is to participate in a way of living in which many people are engaged. The language I speak gets its meaning from the common ways of acting and responding to many people. I take part in a language in the sense in which I take part in a game – which is surely one reason why Wittgenstein compares languages to games. Another reason for this comparison is that in both languages

and games there are rules. To follow the rules for the use of an expression is nothing other than to use the expression as it is ordinarily used – which is to say, as it is used by those many people who take part in the activities in which the expression is embedded. Thus the meaning of the expression is independent of me, or of any particular person; and this is why I can use the expression correctly or incorrectly. It has a meaning independent of my use of it. And this is why there is no sense in the supposition that a forever-solitary person could know a language any more than he could buy and sell. (*Inquiry*, 1989, p. 22)

Wittgenstein's point is that any rule can be understood by anyone, and therefore is public. So no linguistic system can be private in the Cartesian sense, i.e., private in principle. Moreover, because every language is rule-governed, mistakes in the application of its rules are always possible. If there were a 'private language' the distinction between correctly and incorrectly following a rule would make no sense. There would be no objective way of determining, for example, when a mistake in usage had been made. Hence the Cartesian conception is not a language at all. It follows, more generally from this linguistic analogy, that the Cartesian model does not generate a sensible picture of the relationship of the human mind to the external world. One lives in a public world where one learns to use language in accordance with the prevailing social uses of words. These practices instruct us in how to use terms applying to such things as tables, other persons, astral bodies, and various institutions. If the Cartesian model were correct we could never acquire knowledge of such external objects. But since we do have such knowledge it is drastically mistaken. In effect, Wittgenstein is reiterating his great new idea: to understand what the world is like we must scrutinize it. The Cartesian theory rejects such advice. It is an example of a theorist's thinking about but not looking closely at what goes on.

On Certainty

Wittgenstein and Moore

In *On Certainty* we find a new stage in Wittgenstein's philosophical growth. This development is not a change in his descriptive method, with its emphasis on ordinary language. On the contrary. For the rest of his career he remained committed to the method, i.e., to the notion that in order to resolve philosophical problems one must 'look closely at what goes on.' The method is used, almost without variation, in the *Blue* and *Brown Books* (1933–1935); *Philosophical Investigations*, the longest portion of which (Part I) was completed in 1936; *Zettel*, a collection of clippings, most of them written between 1945 and 1948; and *Remarks on Colour*; *Last Writings on the Philosophy of Psychology*; and *On Certainty*, all produced in the last two years of his life. *On Certainty* contains his final thoughts. The last seven entries were inserted in the text only two days before his death on 29 April 1951.

In fact, it was Wittgenstein's emphasis upon description that led him to his third great idea, a remarkable discovery connected with the concept of a language-game. As we noted in the previous chapter, by a language-game Wittgenstein means a slice of human activity, such as giving orders, reporting an event, forming and testing a hypothesis, play-acting, making and telling a joke, solving a problem in practical arithmetic, and so forth. But in *On Certainty* his descriptive focus results in a new insight: that every such game rests on a foundation (or ground) that is certain. His book is thus a new and original account of the nature of certainty. Its main idea is that certainty is to be identified with what is foundational, i.e., with the ground or grounds (he uses both the singular and plural in this connection) that underlie and support a language-game. A corollary of this point is that certain epistemic concepts, such as knowing, doubting, believing, justifying, adducing evidence for or against a claim, truth, falsity, and being mistaken, have their use or uses within language-games but are inapplicable to what is foundational. Instead, they 'come to an end' in the language-game:

> Giving grounds, however, justifying the evidence, comes to an end – but the end is not certain propositions' striking us immediately as true, i.e., it is not a kind of *seeing* on our part; it is our *acting* which lies at the bottom of the language-game. (*On Certainty*, 204)
>
> If the true is what is grounded, then the ground is not *true*, nor yet false. (*On Certainty*, 205)

But if the ground or foundation is 'not true nor yet false,' neither known nor not known, neither justifiable nor unjustifiable, neither confirmable nor infirmable, then it is beyond revision; and that is simply another way of saying that it is certain. What he is getting at is captured in the following passage:

> Isn't the question this: 'What if you had to change your opinion even on these most fundamental things?' And to that the answer seems to me to be: 'You don't *have* to change it. That is just what their being "fundamental" is.' (*On Certainty*, 512)

The twin discoveries that such certain foundations exist and that no epistemic notions apply to them constitute Wittgenstein's new great idea. These findings are without parallel in previous philosophy, including his own. This is an an enormous achievement. Whether certainty is attainable is a problem that has bedevilled thinkers from the time of the Greeks to the present. Nearly every great philosopher – Plato, Descartes, and Kant, just to mention a few – has grappled with the issue. But nobody was able to come up with Wittgenstein's solution. It is not only original, but complicated and the rest of the chapter will be devoted to it.

The story of how Wittgenstein came to write *On Certainty* is both fascinating in itself and highly relevant in understanding the development of this new idea. In 1949, shortly before he was diagnosed with cancer of the prostate, Wittgenstein visited his former student Norman Malcolm in Cornell. Some years earlier Malcolm had written an article, 'Moore and Ordinary Language,' for an anthology entitled *The Philosophy of G. E. Moore* (1942). In that essay, Malcolm argued that Moore's famous defense of the common sense view of the world was really a defense of ordinary language against the extended and paradoxical uses of its locutions by philosophers. As Malcolm wrote:

> Moore's great historical role consists in the fact that he has been perhaps the first philosopher to sense that any philosophical statement which violates ordinary language is false, and consistently to defend ordinary language against its philosophical violators. (368)

But in the intervening seven-year period Malcolm had changed his mind. He now believed that in 'A Defense of Common Sense,' 'Proof of an External World,' and 'Certainty,' Moore had also misused the idioms 'I know,' 'I know with certainty,' 'It is certain,' and 'I have conclusive evidence.' In a paper, 'Defending Common Sense,' that was soon to be published in *The Philosophical Review* he gave a number of powerful arguments in support of this interpretation. Here, in part, is what he said:

> The first respect, therefore, in which Moore's usage of the expression 'I know' in the philosophical contexts we are considering, departs from ordinary usage is that Moore says: 'I know that so and so is true' in circumstances where no one doubts that so and so is true and where there is not even any question as to whether so and so is true. It will be objected: 'His opponent has a philosophical doubt as to whether so and so is true, and there is a philosophical question as to whether so and so is true.' That is indeed the case. What I am saying is that the philosophical doubt and the philosophical question are raised in circumstances in which there isn't any doubt and isn't any

123

question as to whether so and so is true. Moore's opponent would not raise a philosophical question as to whether it is certain that an object before them is a tree if the object were largely obscured or too distant to be easily seen. If he said 'I wish to argue that it isn't certain that that object is a tree' and Moore replied 'I can't tell at this distance whether it is a tree or a bush,' then Moore's opponent would change the example. He would not want to use as an example for his philosophical argument an object with regard to which there was some doubt as to whether it was a tree. The use of an object as an example for presenting his philosophical doubt is spoiled for him if there is any doubt as to what the object is. It must be the case that there is no doubt that the given object is a tree before he can even raise a philosophical question as to whether it is certain that it is a tree. (204–205)

When Wittgenstein arrived in Cornell, Malcolm read him this paper. Wittgenstein had long been interested in Moore's defense of the common sense view of the world, and had even told Moore that 'A Defense of Common Sense' was his best paper. Wittgenstein was thus impressed by Malcolm's claim that Moore was misusing such expressions as 'I know that,' 'I know that with certainty,' etc. When he returned to England, he decided to look into the matter himself, and began to write in his characteristically diffuse style about the correct use of these expressions and then more extensively about the topic of certainty itself. The material we have that his editors subsequently entitled *On Certainty* is in first draft form and unpolished, with all of the later entries dated by groups. It thus allows one to follow the progress of Wittgenstein's thought on this topic in the last two years of his life. The progression shows a deepening sensitivity to its complexities. This work begins with the sort of issues about Moore's use of 'I know' that Malcolm had raised; the influence of Malcolm's paper on Wittgenstein is patent. For instance, in the sixth entry, Wittgenstein writes:

Now, can one enumerate what one knows (like Moore)? Straight off like that, I believe not – For otherwise the expression 'I know' gets misused. And through this misuse a queer and extremely important mental state seems to be revealed.

But Wittgenstein was to carry the issues surrounding the notion of certainty much farther than either Malcolm or Moore, and it is in the depth and originality of his inquiry that the importance of *On Certainty* lies. The outcome of that inquiry was a philosophical masterpiece comparable to the *Tractatus* and the *Investigations*.

In particular, what did he find so provocative and challenging in Moore's essays? I think there are two things, each of which will take some time to relate.

First: In contrast to the rampant scientism, relativism, and pragmatism in twentieth-century philosophy, typified by W. V. O. Quine's naturalized epistemology which holds that philosophy is just an extension of science, or even more radical variants that deny it any descriptive validity whatever, Moore presents a powerful defense of its autonomy. In his view it is capable of providing a true and unique description of the world. This account, which he calls *The Common Sense View of the World*, is not only different from anything that science informs us about reality, but moreover, is not revisable by the findings of any discipline, whether scientific or otherwise. Indeed, Moore's position is that this pre-technical, pre-scientific outlook that all of us share is deeper, more primitive, and conceptually prior to the refined descriptions of reality that science provides; and accordingly, that any scientific discovery must be compatible with the Common Sense View. Moore's papers thus give us a different picture of the world: one that is both familiar and compelling. A simple example of a proposition that is part of the Common Sense View: *the earth now exists and has existed for a long time.* This is a proposition that virtually every adult knows to be true, but it is not a proposition belonging to science or to any of the humanistic disciplines. There is no department in any university whose inquiries are directed to finding out whether the earth exists. Nor is it an assumption that might turn out to be wrong. It is not something scientists merely assume as a hypothesis; rather, they like everybody else know it to be true. No theory, scientific or otherwise, that denied such a proposition would be rationally defensible; and that in effect is what it means to say that the view is not open to revision. A larger, indefinite list of such propositions is what Moore meant by the common sense view of the world. To some extent Wittgenstein agreed, though with important qualifications, that some 'propositions' – which he named 'hinge propositions' – are not open to doubt and hence are not revisable. So though neither thinker denigrated science, each was asserting that philosophy can provide an alternative to the strictly scientific picture of the world. This is one reason why Wittgenstein thought Moore's epistemological writings were worth serious study. But in stressing their concurrence one must add that their accounts of certainty were to differ radically.

Second: In Moore's writings on certainty, we find one of the two major contemporary alternatives to what is today the most commonly received theory of knowledge: a theory that received an explicit formulation in Hume (1711–1776) and has been widely accepted since. It amounts to a mitigated form of skepticism, and it is this view that Moore challenged. In *On Certainty*, Wittgenstein was to join forces with Moore, but in a more original and more profound way.

According to this 'official theory' all knowledge claims are expressible as propositions that fall into two categories that are *exclusive* and *exhaustive*. To say that the categories are exclusive means that no proposition can be a member of both, and to say they are exhaustive means that they include all instances of knowledge claims. We thus have a synoptic theory covering all possible cases. One of the complications in describing the theory is exactly how these contrasting categories are to be defined or characterized.

Historically, there have been different names and frequently different conceptions associated with each. For instance, Hume himself distinguished between propositions expressing a relationship of ideas to one another and propositions about matters of fact. In Leibniz there is a related, though different, distinction: that between necessary and contingent propositions. Kant discriminated between analytic and synthetic propositions. Both Kant and Hume distinguished a priori from a posteriori propositions. In the twentieth century, we find philosophers employing all of the above plus other discriminations: L-determinate versus F-determinate propositions, tautologies versus significant propositions, empirical versus logical propositions, and so on. In a longer essay, each of these different pairs would have to be distinguished from one another. For instance, to say that a proposition is necessary is not identical with saying that it is analytic. To say the former is to say that the proposition holds (is true) in all possible worlds; to say the latter is to say that the predicate term is part of the meaning of the subject term and in that sense gives us a (partial) analysis of the meaning of the subject term. Some philosophers have maintained that 'Every event has a cause' is necessary because it holds in all possible worlds, but that it is not analytic because 'being caused' is not part of the meaning of 'event.' Some propositions, however, are both analytic and necessary, for instance 'All husbands are married.' It is necessary because it is true in all possible worlds, and it is analytic because 'being married' is part of the meaning of 'being a husband.' Similar differences hold between the other pairs of notions I have mentioned.

But historically, all of the propositions belonging to the a priori (necessary, analytical, L-determinate, tautological) side of the distinction have been thought to possess an important epistemological characteristic that marks them off from those belonging to the a posteriori (synthetic, empirical, contingent) side of the distinction. The characteristic is that they can be determined to be true without any reference to experience. The operative point can be brought out by considering how we come to establish the truth of the following propositions:

(i)   All husbands are married.
(ii) All present-day laptop computers weigh less than 20 pounds.

It is clear that at some relevant time in the past we could only have determined whether (ii) is true by an appeal to experience, i.e., by investigating the weights of laptop computers, or by checking the production records of manufacturers, say. The point is that in order to determine the truth of (ii) some research would be requisite. It is not enough merely to have understood the proposition. This is what it means to say that (ii) is a posteriori; namely, that its truth can be ascertained only after some resort to experience. This proposition also has the feature that it might have been false: one can imagine that a certain firm made some heavy, experimental laptops it did not sell to the public. So to say that (ii) might have been false is equivalent to saying that it is not a necessary truth, since there are imaginable circumstances in which it might not have been true. But now let us contrast (ii) with (i). We can tell without any research that (i) is true. We know this prior to any sort of investigation of the facts of the matter. All we have to do is to understand the proposition and we can see that it is true. Moreover, it is not merely true; it is necessarily true. For it is impossible to imagine or describe any circumstances in which, as those terms are customarily used, someone could be a husband without being married. So (i) is both a priori and necessary.

Now Hume and many subsequent philosophers saw this exclusive-exhaustive division, however it was expressed, as having important and highly paradoxical implications for the theory of knowledge. They contended that propositions belonging to the category of the a posteriori (synthetic, contingent, etc.) were never certain and they bolstered this inference with the argument that all such propositions could be determined to be true only on the basis of past experience; and since past experience, being only a sample of all experience, might turn out in the light of future happenings to have been unreliable, such propositions could never be certain. At most they could be known to be true with some degree of probability. In contrast, a priori (analytic, necessary, tautological) propositions are certain. To say that they are 'certain' entails that they hold in all possible circumstances, so that no future experience can run counter to them, and in this in turn entails that a person asserting them cannot be mistaken. But such certitude produced no information about the world; it was a product of the special, usually definitional, relationships holding between the terms in a proposition. From the truth of the sentence 'All giants are tall,' it does not follow that there are giants. Or as Wittgenstein pointed out, one who knows that it will either rain or not rain knows nothing about the weather. Such propositions thus provide information about conceptual relationships, not about matters of fact. Accordingly, this Humean analysis issued in a paradox about knowledge, namely that insofar as propositions are descriptive of the world they can never be certain; and insofar as they are certain they are devoid of information about the world. The theory thus supported a kind of skepticism since it maintained that one could never have information about the world that was certain.

In the twentieth century, this Humean theory has had two major challenges, one from Moore, the other from Quine, both having important implications for epistemology. In 'Two Dogmas of Empiricism' (1950), Quine argued that the difference between so-called 'synthetic propositions' and so-called 'analytic propositions' is a difference of degree, not of kind. According to him all propositions are in principle susceptible to modification or even rejection in the light of new discoveries; they merely differ in the degree of their susceptibility to such changes. For example, the basic laws of logic and physics are less vulnerable to revision than scientific conjectures, but in principle any proposition, even a law of logic, may be abandoned or altered depending on how it fares in confrontation with experience. It seems a straight implication from such an analysis that there is no such thing as absolute certainty, since any proposition that is certain will hold come what may.

But Moore's challenge was of a completely different order. He thought, unlike Quine, that the traditional distinction in kind between contingent and necessary propositions was defensible. What he denied in 'A Defense of Common Sense,' 'Proof of an External World,' and 'Certainty,' was that contingent propositions could not be known to be true with absolute certainty. Indeed, he asserted the exact opposite: for instance, that he knew such empirical propositions as 'I am a human being' (said about himself) and 'The earth has existed for many years past,' to be true with certainty. Though Moore does not explicitly mention that Hume is his target, in effect he was issuing a profound challenge to the official theory deriving from his eighteenth-century predecessor, and of course to its skeptical underpinnings. It was his contention that contingent propositions can be certain that Wittgenstein found attractive. But to find a thesis attractive is not to find it right. Wittgenstein's account of the nature of certainty was to differ substantially from Moore's. And why it did is the key to understanding *On Certainty*. To make this possible, I will divide my discussion into five parts: (1) Foundationalism and certitude, (2) The 'propositional' and 'non-propositional' accounts of certainty, (3) Why doubting must come to an end, (4) The Cartesian Dream Hypothesis, and (5) Skepticism.

Foundationalism and certitude

What is foundationalism? This is a question that needs to be addressed before we discuss Wittgenstein's views. All proponents of the doctrine identify the foundational with certainty. There are many different versions of the position. Wittgenstein's in particular differs from any other in the history of philosophy and also has the merit of avoiding many of its traditional liabilities. His description of the foundational is usually couched in metaphorical language. He speaks of the 'scaffolding of our thoughts,' 'bedrock,' 'the substratum of all my inquiring and asserting,' 'hard rock,' 'being anchored,' and 'hinges.' He says with respect to hinges, 'If I want the door to turn, the hinges must stand fast.' Wittgenstein uses a range of German expressions for certainty, among them 'feststehen,' 'festhalten,' and 'festlegen,' which are usually translated into English as 'standing fast.' Thus when he states that something 'stands fast for us,' he means that it is certain. To bring out how his foundationalism differs from all other versions, I shall start with a simple conceptual model that every foundationalist accepts, including Wittgenstein. The model is so simple and so general that it will lack the cognitive substance that has distinguished traditional foundationalists from one another. But it does capture certain formal features that can be used as the basis for such discriminations.

From at least the time of Aristotle many philosophers have asserted that some of the knowledge human beings possess is more fundamental or basic than the rest. If we call such primordial knowledge 'F' and the remainder 'R,' we can roughly express their intuition by saying that R depends on F but not conversely and that F depends on nothing. What is driving this intuition can be indicated with a brief example. Suppose one were to ask a philosopher: 'What holds up the world?' and the response was 'an elephant.' One might then ask: 'Well, what holds up the elephant?' Suppose the philosopher answers: 'Another elephant.' If such questions and answers were to go on indefinitely nothing would have been explained. Indeed, the philosopher's statements amount to a kind of absurdity. Unless there is something solid that ultimately holds up an elephant it cannot hold up anything. An infinite regress thus turns out to be no explanation at all. So we need a solid foundation (i.e., certitude) that is unsupported by anything else if we are to explain how we come to have knowledge. This is the kind of intuition that has motivated classical forms of foundationalism.

Historically there have been many forms of foundationalism: in epistemology, in ethics, and in logic, for example. What each of these differing forms of foundationalism takes to be fundamental will depend on the particular discipline: in epistemology, for example, it will be a special piece of propositional knowledge, something 'seen' immediately to be true. Descartes thought that the proposition 'cogito ergo sum' (I think, therefore I am) – the so-called 'cogito' – was a piece of such knowledge. One can 'see' clearly and distinctly that if one is thinking then one exists. Starting from such a palpable truth he then showed how the remaining edifice of knowledge could be constructed from it as a base. In ethics, J. S. Mill's *Principle of Utility* is such a fundamental principle. In mathematical logic the axioms play comparable roles. In order to understand what foundationalism is, however, we should move away from any particular theory and uncover its basic conceptual structure. This is something that all forms of foundationalism share.

Let us therefore leave F and R uninterpreted and not take them to be instances of knowledge, morality, or logic. What remains is just a formal structure. It holds that there is some asymmetrical relationship of dependence between F and R, whatever these are taken to be, and that F is not dependent on anything else. So given some unanalyzed notion of 'dependence' and some unanalyzed conception of what F and R may be, we can say that this skeleton gives us the basic foundationlist conception. The main thrust of the model is that F somehow supports R and is itself not supported by anything else. The idea that F is unsupported is generally taken to be another way of saying that it is both basic and certain.

Still, if we want the model, even in this skeletel form, to be adequate to the historical tradition that begins with the Greeks we shall have to add another element to it. It is difficult to state this without giving specific examples, so some examples will follow. The idea is that F will be either a single thing or a very limited number of things if there is more than one F, whereas R will be complex, possessing scope and amplitude. The foundationalist picture thus depicts a particular discipline as having topologically the shape of an inverted pyramid. The main body of this top-heavy structure will rest on a simple base. Its apex will be broader than its base. We can call the base the foundation and what rests on it the mansion. In the realm of philosophy there are many mansions that conform to this model. A typical example would be an axiomatic logical system, such as that developed by Whitehead and Russell in *Principia Mathematica*. As is well known, the system rests on a set of primitives, five axioms that define them, and a principle of inference. This is the base of the system that expands upward and outward, forming a logical mansion that eventually allowed Russell and Whitehead to derive Peano's Postulates from a set of ascending calculi. Some years later, H. M. Sheffer showed that the five axioms could be reduced to one, thus simplifying the base. The resulting picture was that of an inverted pyramid, with the sentential calculus being derived from the axioms, the predicate calculus later, and so on. One can think of the Cartesian philosophy as giving rise to a parallel image, whose elements are not logical theorems but ordinary epistemic propositions. Their base is the cogito – the F or foundation. The totality of propositions forming the mansion is R; these are propositions that Descartes claimed could be derived from F.

Now a final example from ethics. Suppose one holds that cheating is always wrong, and suppose that a moral skeptic challenges this claim. One may defend his position in one of two ways. He may argue that the prohibition against cheating is a basic principle of morality, and that nothing further can be said in its behalf. Or if he holds that it is not basic, he will claim that it can be derived from a deeper principle. Suppose the deeper principle in this case is the Principle of Utility. This principle entails that cheating is wrong because in the long run it will lead to a preponderance of unhappiness over happiness. If the skeptic now challenges the Principle of Utility, a proponent of the thesis again has two options. He can claim that it is basic or that it rests upon a still deeper principle. The eventual outcome of the process of responding to obsessive challenge is a form of foundationalism that asserts that all moral reasoning ultimately rests on a principle that lies beyond justification or evidential support.

Even in this skeletel form, the model needs some further explanation. For example, what does it mean to say that F depends on nothing whatever? Consider the cogito for a moment. It is the foundation of an epistemic superstructure. The items belonging to the superstructure are said to depend on the foundational item. Let us agree that the dependence runs in the way that Descartes indicates. The important point to notice is that the cogito itself is a piece of knowledge. Descartes is saying, in effect, that the notion of 'dependence' applies to and is limited to putative pieces of knowledge. So F and R must be instances of knowledge before the notion of dependence can be sensibly applied to their relationship. Given this condition, his thesis would be that F does not depend on any piece of knowledge in order to be a piece of knowledge. That is what it means to say it is fundamental. Again, in a different domain of philosophy, Mill might have responded in the same way. Like such moral principles as equal crimes deserve equal punishment, the Principle of Utility is itself a moral principle. Nearly all classical forms of foundationalism thus assume that F is a specimen exactly like those that belong to R. The main difference is that it is fundamental and they are not.

This line of reasoning brings us to Wittgenstein, and to the major respect in which he differs from the Western tradition. As we have seen, he rejects the idea that what is foundational is susceptible to doubt, proof, confirmation, truth, falsity, or justification. These attributes apply to putative cases of knowledge but not to what is certain. Whatever is so susceptible belongs to the language-game and differs in kind from the ground that underlies it. As he says: '"Knowledge" and "certainty" belong to different categories. They are not two "mental states" like, say, "surmising" and "being sure."' (*On Certainty*, 308). The base and the mansion resting on it are thus logically divergent. In saying this he realized that he was saying something philosophically insightful about the entire epistemological tradition. It is Wittgenstein's rejection of the notion of categorial similarity between base and mansion that, to a great extent, separates him from that tradition and from Moore.

As I mentioned above, Wittgenstein's form of foundationalism is not only unique but it enables him to avoid a set of obdurate problems that have perplexed nearly all varieties of foundationalism.

What are these problems? They arise from a set of questions that are meat for the skeptic. According to the tradition, foundational F is said to be more fundamental than any R. But the skeptic will ask: How do you know that? How can you be sure that there isn't something more fundamental than F upon which it depends?

A variety of answers have historically been given to this question. Descartes stated that he could 'see clearly and distinctly' that the cogito was true. Others have answered that unless some F were known to be true we would be committed to an infinite regress like that of insisting that an elephant holds up the world.

Wittgenstein, as a foundationalist, also asserts that nothing could be more certain than that which stands fast for us, but given his form of foundationalism the regress problem does not arise. It arises for traditional epistemologists because they assume that the question 'How do you know that F is true?' is always applicable. And they assume that because they think that the foundation and what rests on it belong to the same category, i.e., that both are pieces of knowledge. But for Wittgenstein's form of foundationalism, the question is not applicable and in fact embodies a category mistake. One cannot sensibly ask of that which is certain whether it is known (or not known) or true (or false); for what is meant by certitude is not susceptible to such ascriptions. As we noted earlier, he says: 'If the true is what is grounded, then the ground is not *true*, nor yet false.' The skeptical question thus need not be answered. This shows again how radically his view differs from any conventional form of foundationalism.

Propositional and non-propositional accounts of certainty

There are two different accounts of F in *On Certainty*. One of these – the earlier – is propositional in character. It derives from Wittgenstein's response to Moore, who thinks of certainty as applying to a set of empirical propositions that he knows to be true. In contrast, Wittgenstein says that so-called 'hinge propositions' appear to be ordinary empirical propositions but are not. Straightforward empirical propositions, by definition, are either true or false, confirmable or infirmable, etc., but so-called 'hinge propositions' are immune to such ascriptions. He discriminates them from standard empirical propositions in various ways:

> That is to say, the *questions* that we raise and our *doubts* depend on the fact that some propositions are exempt from doubt, as it were like hinges on which those turn. (*On Certainty*, 341)

> When Moore says he *knows* such and such, he is really enumerating a lot of empirical propositions which we affirm without special testing; propositions, that is, which have a peculiar logical role in the system of our empirical propositions. (*On Certainty*, 136)

Thus, what Wittgenstein is calling 'hinge propositions' are not really propositions at all. This is because of the 'peculiar logical role' they play. Later he will try to describe their role or roles. He will call them 'grammatical rules,' 'rules of instruction,' or 'rules of testing.' His so-called 'propositional view' is thus only nominally 'propositional.' It is better described as an account of locutions that look like propositions but function as kinds of rules.

   The second, later account is palpably non-propositional. It is also overtly non-Cartesian. As we recall from an earlier quotation, it denies that certitude consists in propositions at all, let alone propositions that we can *see* to be true.

> Giving grounds, however, justifying the evidence, comes to an end; – but the end is not certain propositions striking us immediately as true, i.e., it is not a kind of *seeing* on our part; it is our *acting* which lies at the bottom of the language game. (*On Certainty*, 204)

Let us now look at both accounts to see how they resemble and differ. I shall begin with the 'propositional' version. It is marked by two characteristics: (i) that foundational propositions form a system, and (ii) that such foundations do not stand absolutely but only relatively fast. In both respects, Wittgenstein differs from Descartes who thinks of the cogito as the *sole* foundational item and from Moore whose common sense propositions do not form a system; and from both Descartes and Moore who think that their foundational propositions stand fast independently of any circumstances in which they are asserted. The notion that hinge propositions form a system is to be found in the following quotations (which are only a subset of a larger number making the same point).

> What I hold fast to is not *one* proposition but a nest of propositions. (*On Certainty*, 225)

> When we first begin to *believe* anything, what we believe is not a single proposition, it is a whole system of propositions. (Light dawns gradually over the whole.) (*On Certainty*, 141)

> It is not single axioms that strike me as obvious, it is a system in which consequences and premises give one another *mutual* support. (*On Certainty*, 142)

> The child learns to believe a host of things. i.e. it learns to act according to these beliefs. Bit by bit there forms a system of what is believed, and in that system some things stand unshakeably fast and some are more or less liable to shift. What stands fast does so, not because it is intrinsically obvious or convincing; it is rather held fast by what lies around it. (*On Certainty*, 144)

This last quotation denies that what stands fast does so because it is 'intrinsically obvious.' This is Wittgenstein's way of disassociating himself from Cartesian foundationalism. Here are two quotations that evince his relativism:

> It might be imagined that some propositions, of the form of empirical propositions, were hardened and functioned as channels for such empirical propositions as were not hardened but fluid; and that this relation altered with time, in that fluid propositions hardened, and hard ones became fluid. (*On Certainty*, 96)

> But if someone were to say 'So logic too is an empirical science,' he would be wrong. Yet this is right: the same proposition may get treated at one time as something to test by experience, at another as a rule of testing. (*On Certainty*, 98)

Thus, a proposition that stands fast at a given time may not stand fast at another. When it stands fast it is a 'hinge proposition,' and when it no longer stands fast it ceases to be one. Wittgenstein compares propositions to pieces of apparatus. When we are surveying the night sky with a telescope, the instrument does not come under scrutiny; it stands fast in those circumstances. In that context it is like a hinge proposition. But if something goes awry, we may wish to examine the optical device itself. In that case it no longer stands fast but instead has become an object of inquiry. In such a case something else must stand fast if one is to make a proper examination of the telescope. Standing fast is thus relativized to context: a proposition is not intrinsically certain, but it is held fast by what surrounds it.

His later non-propositional view, by way of contrast, is both absolutistic and non-systematic. Wittgenstein did not have this idea in mind when he began to write the notes that comprise *On Certainty*, probably because his focus was on Moore's texts, with their propositional emphasis. It is also probable that he was influenced by Malcolm's paper 'Defending Common Sense,' which attacks Moore's use of 'I know' and which Malcolm read to him in 1949. But as the work proceeds, the second view begins to emerge. The first slowly recedes and is then replaced. Like many views that are developed in opposition to another, his second account of certainty takes different forms, depending on the particular contrast Wittgenstein wishes to highlight. There are three main forms: (i) that certainty is something primitive, instinctual, or animal, (ii) that it is acting, and (iii) that it derives from rote training in communal practices. In all of these the major contrast with the propositional view is his denial that what stands fast is the product of reasoning or intellection. Here are some citations that mention these three strands:

> I want to regard man here as an animal; as a primitive being to which one grants instinct but not ratiocination. As a creature in a primitive state … Language did not emerge from some kind of ratiocination. (*On Certainty*, 475)

> … it is our *acting* which lies at the bottom of the language-game. (*On Certainty*, 204)

> The child, I should like to say, learns to react in such-and-such a way; and in so reacting it doesn't so far know anything. Knowing only begins at a later level. (*On Certainty*, 538)

> From a child up I learnt to judge like this. *This is* judging. (*On Certainty*, 128)

> 'We are quite sure of it' does not mean just that every single person is certain of it, but that we belong to a community which is bound together by science and education. (*On Certainty*, 298)

These three strands – instinct, acting, training – are different. If they were to be analysed further, which Wittgenstein of course never had time to do, they might well turn out (as I believe) to be in tension with one another. But I think that Wittgenstein meant them to be part of a single complex idea that he wishes to contrast with the propositional account. It is thus possible to find an interpretation that welds them into a single (admittedly complex) conception of that which stands fast. On this interpretation, what Wittgenstein takes to be foundational is a picture of the world we all inherit as members of a human community. We have been trained from birth in ways of acting that are non-reflective to accept a picture of the world that is ruthlessly realistic: that there is an earth, persons on it, objects in our environment, and so forth. This picture is manifested in action. When we open a door our lives show that we are certain. Certainty is thus not a matter of theorizing about opening the door but an unreflective, instinctive way of acting with respect to it.

All animals, including humans, inherit their picture of the world and like other animals much of our inheritance derives from early training –'something must be taught us as a foundation' (*On Certainty*, 449). It is no accident that the reference to children plays such a prominent role in the later sections of the text. 'For how can a child immediately doubt what it is taught? That could mean only that he was incapable of learning certain language-games' (*On Certainty*, 283). 'We teach a child "that is your hand", not "that is perhaps (or 'probably') your hand". That is how a child learns the innumerable language-games that are concerned with his hand … Nor, on the other hand, does he learn that he *knows* this is a hand' (*On Certainty*, 374). 'Children do not learn that books exist, that armchairs exist, etc., etc., – they learn to fetch books, sit in armchairs, etc. etc.' (*On Certainty*, 476). 'So is this it: I must recognize certain authorities in order to make judgments at all?' (*On Certainty*, 493).

In these passages we see an explicit rejection of the notion that what stands fast for us is the product of reason and ratiocination. The foundations are neither known nor unknown, neither reasonable nor unreasonable. They are there, just like our lives. But in the preceding passages the examples he gives make it clear that his foundationalism is non-relative. The existence of the earth and the communities which nurture us are not like pieces of apparatus that can be discarded or repaired if they do not work correctly. The notion of 'working correctly' has no application to these cases. We cannot revise, alter, or question the existence of the earth. It and the communities that live on it stand absolutely fast. In both the propositional and non-propositional accounts the method of 'looking closely at what goes on' is followed rigorously. 'At some point,' he writes in *On Certainty*, 189, 'one has to pass from explanation to mere description.' 'Somewhere we must be finished with justification, and then there remains the proposition that this is how we calculate' (*On Certainty*, 212). It is this powerful descriptive account that tells us why in principle doubting must terminate, and, accordingly, why the Cartesian Dream Hypothesis and its resulting skepticism are both nonsensical.

Why doubting must come to an end

From the *Tractatus* on, Wittgenstein held that philosophical perplexity arises because we do not understand the 'logic of our language.' Of course, in that early work he meant by 'logic' the formal language that Whitehead and Russell had developed in *Principia Mathematica*. But in his later philosophy this conception was abandoned. Now not understanding the logic of our language means not understanding a kind of informal logic to be found in everyday discourse. These remarks embed at least four different, but increasingly sophisticated, conceptions. First, there is the explicit notion that such a lack of understanding will give rise to conceptual puzzles and perplexities. Second, this notion implies that if we *do* understand the logic of our language such perplexities will not arise. This second position has textual support in such remarks as:

> And this description gets its light, that is to say its purpose, from the philosophical problems. These are, of course, not empirical problems; they are solved, rather, by looking into the workings of our language, and that in such a way as to make us recognize those workings: *in despite of* an urge to misunderstand them. The problems are solved, not by giving new information, but by arranging what we have always known. Philosophy is a battle against the bewitchment of our intelligence by means of language. (*Philosophical Investigations*, 109)

Third, this quotation and others like it indicate that Wittgenstein is operating at two levels: describing how language actually works and describing, via language, how the world is. If we get clear about language we can then 'see the world rightly.' In other words, Wittgenstein is not merely speaking about the differences in the uses of such terms as 'believe,' 'know,' 'certain,' 'evidence,' 'justification,' and 'doubt' (though he is certainly doing that as well) but also about that which those words normally denote or pick out, that is, about belief, knowledge, certainty and doubt. These are features we find in everyday human life; that is, people believe, doubt, justify and provide evidence for or against various claims. It is these features of human activity that primarily interest Wittgenstein. Language is important because it is *the* medium for giving us an accurate picture of 'what goes on.' But it can do this only if we *command a clear view* of the use of our words, as he puts it.

This brings us to our fourth point, namely that in his later philosophy he is using 'logic' in a new, non-traditional way. He now means that each word in everyday language has a restricted range of application. But it follows from his two-level approach that this entails that the activities themselves are circumscribed by rule-governed boundaries. It is these boundaries that determine when an activity makes sense. There is a parallel at the linguistic level. If words are stretched beyond their normal limits they cease to make sense. Thus one can use words correctly and one can use them incorrectly. To say that they are used correctly means that they conform to the way that native speakers use them in the language-game. Philosophers tend to use these words incorrectly and when they do bewilderment is the consequence. Wittgenstein's dual approach arrives at profound insights both about language and human activity. Consider doubting, for instance. This is an everyday practice that has its limits. These limits are defined by de facto rules that govern what actually takes place in the language game. As Wittgenstein puts it, 'these rules ... only make sense if they come to an end somewhere.' There are many passages in *On Certainty* to the same effect:

> If you tried to doubt everything you would not get as far as doubting anything. (*On Certainty*, 115)

> A doubt without an end is not even a doubt. (*On Certainty*, 625)

> Doubting has certain characteristic manifestations, but they are only characteristic of it in particular circumstances. If someone said that he doubted the existence of his hands, kept looking at them from all sides, tried to make sure it wasn't 'all done by mirrors', etc. we should not be sure whether we ought to call that doubting. We might describe his way of behaving as like the behavior of doubt, but his game would not be ours. (*On Certainty*, 255)

This last quotation is especially important. In saying that doubting has characteristic manifestations but *only in particular circumstances*, Wittgenstein is calling attention to the limited nature of such a practice. In giving the example of one who claims to doubt the existence of his hands, he is making an additional point, namely that such extreme behavior is not a case of doubt. Whatever 'game' that person is playing it is not the game of doubting. His point is that philosophers, like Descartes and Moore, are playing a similar game and thus misdescribing the nature of doubt. In fact, the game they are playing is senseless. He describes why this is so by means of a wonderful example:

> It would be as if someone were looking for some object in a room; he opens a drawer and doesn't see it there, then he closes it again, waits, and opens it once more to see if perhaps it isn't there now, and keeps on like that. He has not learned to look for things ... He has not learned *the* game we are trying to teach him. (*On Certainty*, 315)

The person who keeps looking in a drawer, opening and closing it again and again, searching for a missing object, say a cuff link, has not learned how to look for things. He has not learned the game of searching. How could one be taught that game? Roughly speaking, the answer is by early training, by living in a family as part of a community in which people search for lost objects. One comes to learn as a result of such training that it is *senseless* to continue to open and close a drawer obsessively; nothing can be gained after the first few tries. It is like checking the date by looking at hundreds of copies of the same newspaper. Such an obsessive process lacks a procedure for closure. It is senseless because doubt must come to an end.

This example in effect distinguishes cases of doubting from cases of *philosophical doubt*. The word 'doubt' is used both in ordinary speech and in philosophy, but it is essentially a homonym describing two entirely different activities, one of them sensible, the other not. The skeptic who doubts obsessively is like the person who endlessly opens and closes a drawer, or like one who invokes an endless supply of elephants to explain what holds the world up. The skeptic does not understand that the rules of the language-game require that doubting must come to an end. Real doubting, in contrast, is not open-ended. After some tries to find the missing cuff link one is either successful or abandons the task. This is something that Moore failed to understand and it helps explain why his attempt to rebut skepticism failed.

The Dream Hypothesis

In its simplest form the Cartesian Dream Hypothesis is the claim that one cannot distinguish dream episodes from veridical ones and accordingly that for any moment, T, one can never know with certainty that one is not dreaming. From this it follows that there is no moment, T, when one can be certain that one is apprehending real events and not dream events. If this argument were correct no human being could ever attain certitude about the world. Descartes proposed this hypothesis as a challenge to determine whether there is anything he could know with absolute certainty. His answer was the cogito. It assured him that he could not be mistaken about his own existence. Moore had a different way of dealing with the Dream Scenario. For example, in his famous paper

'Certainty,' he states that while he is speaking he knows many things with certainty: that he is standing up, that he has clothes on, that there is a door in that wall, and so forth. But he admits that he cannot *prove* what he *knows*, i.e., that he cannot prove that he is standing up or that he has clothes on. He said that in order to prove he was standing up he would have to prove he was not dreaming and this he admitted he could not do. Yet he went on to assert that since he knew on that occasion that he was standing up, he knew then that he was not dreaming. He claimed that this argument was at least as good as the skeptic's: if you are dreaming then you cannot know you are standing up.

His rebuttal of the Dream Hypothesis thus turned on the distinction between knowing that proposition and proving that proposition. What is important here is to recognize that Moore assumed that it was a *sensible* demand on the part of the skeptic to prove that one was not dreaming, and therefore his response to this challenge was also sensible. These are just the assumptions that Wittgenstein challenged in his later writings, and especially in *On Certainty*. His overall strategy is to show that both the skeptical position and Moore's response are senseless. Since Moore and his skeptical opponents are both representative of philosophical practice from the time of the Greeks to the present, Wittgenstein's objections go to the very heart of the tradition. He is essentially showing that the standard treatments of dreaming, knowing, and doubting in that tradition are completely skewed. As he says: 'The argument "I may be dreaming" is senseless for this reason: if I am dreaming this remark is being dreamed as well – and indeed it is also being dreamed that these words have any meaning' (*On Certainty*, 383).

I said above that the Dream Hypothesis can be formulated in a brief sentence. Wittgenstein does exactly this in the passage just quoted. He says the hypothesis is expressed in the words 'I may be dreaming.' What he will show is that if these words are taken literally they are senseless. His conclusion is that one does not have to meet the Cartesian conjecture by proving there is an external world as Moore tried to do. All one has to do is to show that the hypothesis cannot be sensibly stated and therefore that there is nothing to rebut. His approach is found in *Zettel* and in *On Certainty*.

What would it be like for someone to tell me with complete serious-ness that he (really) did not know whether he was dreaming or awake? –

Is the following situation possible: Someone says 'I believe I am now dreaming'; he actually wakes up soon afterwards, remembers that utterance in his dream and says 'So I was right!' This narrative can surely only signify: Someone dreamt that he had said he was dreaming.

Imagine an unconscious man (anaesthetized, say) were to say 'I am conscious' – should we say 'He ought to know'?

And if someone talked in his sleep and said 'I am asleep' – should we say 'He's quite right'?

Is someone speaking untruth if he says to me 'I am not conscious'? (And truth if he says it while unconscious? And suppose a parrot says: 'I don't understand a word,' or a gramophone: 'I am only a machine'?) (*Zettel*, 396)

I cannot seriously suppose that I am at this moment dreaming. Someone, who dreaming, says: 'I am dreaming' even if he speaks audibly in doing so, is no more right than if he said in his dream 'it is raining' while it was in fact raining. Even if his dream were actually connected with the noise of the rain. (*On Certainty*, 676)

These passages constitute a *reductio ad absurdum* of the Dream Hypothesis. They show that a person who is sound asleep cannot make sensible assertions about his mental state in such a circum-stance. Wittgenstein's line of reasoning rests on an idea that is basic to his later philosophy: that what counts as a significant utterance depends on the context in which it is made. In a brilliant metaphor he asks us to consider the following scenario:

I might make with my hand the movement I should make if I were holding a hand-saw and sawing through a plank; but would one have any right to call this movement *sawing* out of all context? (It might be something quite different!) (*On Certainty*, 350)

In this last passage, Wittgenstein is, in effect, comparing a person who says 'I may be dreaming,' when normal background conditions are not satisfied, with a man who is making movements one would normally make if one were holding a saw and sawing through a plank, but who at that particular moment is holding no saw and has before him no plank. Wittgenstein asks: 'Would one have any right to call this sawing out of all context?' The answer is obviously no. Whatever the man is doing it is not sawing. The background conditions for sawing – having a saw, a plank, and trying to cut the plank – have not been satisfied. And a man who utters certain words out of all context is making no statement. The background conditions for sensible assertion are, among other things, that a person be fully aware of what his words mean and intend them to make a statement. Accordingly, we can reconstruct Wittgenstein's objection to the Dream Hypothesis as follows:

> Insofar as the S, the skeptic, wishes to make a certain kind of conceptual point – for example, that the attainment of certainty is never possible – the utterance S uses must be a genuine statement. Suppose S utters the words, 'I may be dreaming.' If S is dreaming when he utters these words, the requirement of statement-making is violated. For if S is asleep, S is not aware of what he is saying and accordingly is not intending to say anything. It follows that the Dream Hypothesis can only be expressed if S is fully aware of what he wishes to say and that is possible only if S is awake and knows he is. But if S is awake and knows he is, then his remark 'I may be dreaming,' does not make sense if taken literally. The same objection applies to any generalization of this remark, such as 'It is possible that at any given time no person can be sure that he or she is not dreaming.' Clearly one who says this cannot be asleep at the time he utters this sentence; hence there is at least one time when the speaker will know that he or she is awake. Hence, the Dream Hypothesis cannot be sensibly formulated and accordingly the skeptical challenge cannot get off the ground.

The relevance of this argument to Moore's rebuttal of skepticism, and his famous attempt to prove the existence of the external world, is immediate. If the skeptic's position cannot be coherently stated there is no stain that needs to be wiped off the conceptual table. So to offer a so-called proof by way of refutation, or to assert that one knows that one is standing up as a way of undermining the skeptical hypothesis, is simply to multiply confusion. Moore's response to the skeptic is therefore to be rejected because it rests on the mistaken assumption that the skeptical position is sensible.

Skepticism

In the preceding section we concentrated on the Cartesian Dream Hypothesis and its presupposition that endless doubt is perfectly sensible, and then on Wittgenstein's rejoinder that obsessive doubt is senseless. There are of course many other powerful arguments favoring skepticism and to examine each of these in detail would clearly be impossible here. My own view is that practically all of these arguments turn on the principle that since one might be mistaken in any given case it follows that one might be mistaken in every case. If so, nothing can be certain since every case is subject to doubt. The conclusion reached is radical; it makes no difference what the case is: whether it is the existence of the external world or of other minds or of the veracity of memory – it is subject to doubt.

Wittgenstein's treatment of skepticism as a total doctrine is very subtle in *On Certainty*. One can discriminate at least five different objections he makes to this outlook.

The first is the application of his idea that to see the world rightly we must look closely 'at what goes on.' Following his own maxim, Wittgenstein contests the supposed facts that lead to skepticism. He denies that in fact human beings doubt obsessively. As he says, 'The reasonable man does not have certain doubts' (*On Certainty*, 220); 'a doubt is not necessary even when it is possible' (392); and 'One doubts on specific grounds' (458). Wittgenstein is saying in fact we do not invariably doubt this or that proposition. Wittgenstein is asking the philosopher not to theorize but to look and see what human beings actually do or do not doubt. That they do not doubt some things is significant; it suggests that even within the language-game some things are exempt from doubt.

A second objection is expressed in a variety of ways. It is the notion that what the skeptic is calling doubt is not really a case of doubt. What determines something to be such a case is its conformity to community practice. The skeptic does not engage in any such practice and hence his supposititious worries are not really doubts. The point Wittgenstein is making is here is a practical one: such 'worries' do not apply to and therefore do not affect human life. They do not raise real questions and therefore do not require real answers. One might call them 'spurious doubts,' counterfeit bills that cannot be used to buy real goods. Recall some of the ways he expresses this thought: 'A doubt that doubted everything would not be a doubt' (450), and 'A doubt without an end is not even a doubt' (625). The idea that the skeptic's game is not 'our game' is a way of saying that such doubts make no difference to everyday human life. In Wittgensteinian language, 'they lie apart from the route travelled by human inquiry.' They are thus impotent with respect to any significant investigation carried out by persons playing the language-game, including the scientist.

Third, Wittgenstein explicitly rejects the skeptical leap from any case to every case. He states: 'Our not doubting them all is simply our manner of judging, and therefore of acting' (232). The argument Wittgenstein uses against the move from any case to every case is that it would be equivalent to saying that we have always played a certain game (chess, say) incorrectly. From the fact that one might play a single game incorrectly it does not follow that one might play every game incorrectly. The idea that we might always be mistaken, that we could always be adding incorrectly or playing a familiar game incorrectly, is a special form of nonsense in which the wheels of language spin idly and do no work. Once again, his comment 'our not doubting them all is simply our manner of judging,' takes us back to his basic idea that description should replace explanation. We could not be said to be engaging in the community practice called 'judging' if we were always mistaken. And judging exists. A description of that practice includes, as an essential part, that most judgments are correct. Skepticism thus does not provide an accurate account of human behavior.

Fourth, one of Wittgenstein's deepest criticisms of skepticism stems from the notion that all of us are reared in a community. In this ambience we learn to recognize certain persons, our parents and others, learn to speak a language, and eventually come to participate unselfconsciously in a wide range of human interactions, practices and institutions. Wittgenstein says that such an immersion in the community forms our world picture. This picture is inherited and deeply ingrained: so deeply as to be inexpugnible. There is no possible way that one can reject or revise it. Yet the skeptic wishes to question its existence. But even the form the skeptic's challenge takes – the linguistic format to which it must conform so that another can understand it – presupposes the existence of the community and its linguistic practices. The skeptic's doubts are thus self-defeating. They presuppose the very existence of that which he wishes to challenge as possibly non-existent, namely the inherited societal background which stands fast for all of us. They thus serve only to remind us of that which Wittgenstein has stressed: that there is an unrevisable ground that makes the language-game possible.

Finally, Wittgenstein wishes to emphasize that it is the existence of the earth that is the starting point of belief for every human being. There are thus two different components to our inherited world picture. There is the community, as described above, but there is also what epistemologists, like Moore, would call the material (non-organic) world. It represents the deepest level of certitude, having a kind of priority with respect to the community. For unless the material world existed there would be no human communities. Wittgenstein's foundationalism thus differs from those of the tradition in being striated: there are at least two things that stand absolutely fast for all of us: the material world and the community. Both exhibit a kind of objectivity – an intruding presence – which impinges upon human beings and to which in diverse ways they must conform. Neither aspect is open to obsessive doubt or revision. Wittgenstein's 'solution' to the famous problem concerning the existence of the external world is that no sensible question can be raised with respect to either of these aspects. Their existence is presupposed in any formulation of the problem. Therefore to question their existence, as the skeptic presumably wishes to do, is self-defeating. In even trying to formulate its challenge skepticism initiates the process of its own destruction.

Skepticism is thus not a possible position, resting on or embedding a set of consistent beliefs. Accordingly, no counter-argument to it need be mounted, as Moore thought. If there is a philosophical task it is to show why skepticism is plausible and yet why it is impotent. But the task is not wholly negative. It faces two positive challenges: first, to delineate how the language-game is played: how such terms as 'knowledge,' 'belief,' 'doubt,' 'judgment,' and so forth are actually used, an effort that will include an account of the rules that govern such uses: and second, to describe the ground or grounds that make the language-game possible at all. In *On Certainty* Wittgenstein has done both of these things.

I said at the beginning of this book that a compelling case can be made that Wittgenstein is the greatest modern philosopher. There is no question but that his achievements are of the highest order. One of these is to have demonstrated the self-defeating nature of skepticism. He has shown that what the skeptic wishes to say cannot be said without violating the conversational implicatures that would make the challenge sensible. It follows that there is no position that has to be rebutted – as most of the Western tradition has supposed.

When to this achievement is added the development of three great ideas, a new method, the descriptions of the ways that conceptual models exercise their ineluctable grips upon thinkers, and numerous, accurate characterizations of our everyday linguistic and non-linguistic practices, it is difficult to resist the conclusion that Wittgenstein stands alone in the world of contemporary philosophy.

Select bibliography

Ayer, Alfred J. 1948. *Language, Truth, and Logic.* 2nd edn. London: Gollancz.

Baldwin, Thomas. 1990. *G.E. Moore.* London: Routledge.

Bartley, W. W. III. 1973. *Wittgenstein.* Philadelphia and New York: Lippincott.

Bouwsma, O. K. 1986. *Wittgenstein: Conversations 1949–1951.* Indianapolis: Hackett.

Brenner, William H. 1999. *Wittgenstein's Philosophical Investigations.* Albany: Suny.

Carnap, Rudolf. 1928. *Der Logische Aufbau Der Welt* [*The Logical Construction of the World*]. Berlin-Schlachtensee: Weltkries-Verlag.

—. 1937. *The Logical Syntax of Language.* London: Kegan Paul.

—. 1947. *Meaning and Necessity: A Study in Semantics and Modal Logic.* Chicago: University of Chicago Press.

—. 1963. *The Philosophy of Rudolf Carnap.* Edited by P. A. Schilpp. Chicago and La Salle: Open Court.

Conway, Gertrude. 1989. *Wittgenstein on Foundations.* New Jersey: Atlantic Highlands.

Descartes, René. *Meditations on First Philosophy.* Translated by L. J. Lafleur. Indianapolis: Bobbs-Merrill.

Diamond, Cora. 1991. *The Realistic Spirit.* Cambridge, Mass: MIT Press.

Frege, Gottlob. 1949. '*On Sense and Nominatum*' ['*Über Sinn und Bedeutung,*' *1893*]. In Herbert Feigl and W. Sellars, eds., *Readings in Philosophical Analysis.* New York: Appleton-Century-Crofts.

—. 1960. *Translations from the Philosophical Writings of Gottlob Frege* (by Peter Geach and Max Black). 2nd edn Oxford: Blackwell.

—. 1964. *The Basic Laws of Arithmetic.* Translated and edited with an Introduction by Montgomery Furth. Berkeley: University of California Press.

—. 1996. *Nachgelassene Schriften* [*Posthumous Writings*], translated and with commentary by Richard L. Mendelsohn. *Inquiry*, Vol. 39.

—. 2000. *The Frege Reader.* Edited by Michael Beaney. Oxford: Blackwell.

Garver, Newton and Seung-Chong Lee. 1994. *Derrida and Wittgenstein.* Philadelphia: Temple University Press.

Hacker, P. M. S. 1996. *Wittgenstein's Place in Twentieth-Century Analytic Philosophy.* Oxford: Blackwell.

Hanfling, Oswald. 1989. *Wittgenstein's Later Philosophy.* Albany: Suny.

Hannay, Alastair. 1990. *Human Consciousness.* London: Routledge.

Hilmy, S. 1987. *The Later Wittgenstein: The Emergence of a New Philosophical Method.* Oxford: Blackwell.

McGinn, Marie. 1997. *Wittgenstein.* London: Routledge.

Malcolm, Norman. 1984. *Ludwig Wittgenstein: A Memoir.* New York: Oxford University Press.

—. 1986. *Nothing is Hidden: Wittgenstein's Criticism of his Early Thought.* Oxford: Blackwell.

—. 1989. '*Wittgenstein on Language and Rules.*' *Philosophy.* Vol. 64, 5–28.

Mates, Benson. 1981. *Skeptical Essays.* Chicago: University of Chicago Press.

—. 1996. *The Skeptic Way.* New York: Oxford University Press.

Monk, Ray. 1990. *Ludwig Wittgenstein: The Duty of Genius.* New York: Free Press.

Moore, G. E. 1903. *Principia Ethica.* Cambridge, UK: Cambridge University Press.

—. 1903. '*The Refutation of Idealism.*' *Philosophical Studies.* London: Routledge, 1922.

—. 1942. *The Philosophy of G. E. Moore.* Edited by P. A. Schilpp. Chicago and La Salle: Open Court.

—. 1959. *Philosophical Papers.* London: Allen & Unwin.

—. 1965. '*Visual Sense-Data.*' In *Perceiving, Sensing, and Knowing.* Edited by R. J. Swartz. Berkeley: University of California Press, 130–137.

Pascal, Fania. 1984. '*A Personal Memoir.*' In *Recollections of Wittgenstein.* Edited by Rush Rhees. New York: Oxford University Press, 12–49.

Quine, W. V. O. 1953. *From A Logical Point Of View.* New York: Harper & Row.

—. 1960. *Word and Object.* Cambridge, Mass.: MIT Press.

—. 1969. *'Epistemology Naturalized.'* In *Ontological Relativity and Other Essays.* New York: Columbia University Press.

—. 1974. *The Roots of Reference.* La Salle: Open Court.

—. 1991. *'Two Dogmas in Retrospect.'* In *Canadian Journal of Philosophy,* Vol. 21, *265–274.*

Rescher, Nicholas. 1997. *Profitable Speculations.* Lanham, Md.: Rowman and Littlefield.

Rhees, Rush, ed., 1984. *Recollections of Wittgenstein.* New York: Oxford University Press.

Russell, Bertrand. 1918. *'The Philosophy of Logical Atomism.'* In *Logic and Knowledge: Essays 1901–1950.* Edited by R. C. Marsh. London: Allen & Unwin, 1956, 175–282.

—. 1919. *Introduction to Mathematical Philosophy.* London: Allen & Unwin.

—. 1924. *'Logical Atomism.'* In *Logic and Knowledge: Essays 1901–1950.* Edited by R. C. Marsh. London: Allen & Unwin, 1956, 321–344.

—. 1944. *'My Mental Development.'* The Philosophy of Bertrand Russell. Vol. 1. Edited by P. A. Schilpp. Chicago and La Salle: Open Court.

—. 1956. *Logic and Knowledge: Essays, 1901–1950.* Edited by R. C. Marsh. London: Allen & Unwin.

Russell, Bertrand and Alfred North Whitehead. 1910–1913. *Principia Mathematica.* Cambridge: Cambridge University Press.

Savickey, Beth. 1999. *Wittgenstein's Art of Investigation.* London: Routledge.

Sluga, Hans. 1998. *'What Has History To Do with Me? Wittgenstein and Analytic Philosophy.'* Inquiry. Vol. 41, No. 1, 119–121.

Stebbing, Susan. 1942. *'Moore's Influence.'* In *The Philosophy of G.E. Moore.* Edited by P. A. Schilpp. Chicago and La Salle: Open Court, 515–532.

Stern, David G. 1995. *Wittgenstein on Mind and Language.* New York: Oxford University Press.

—. 2000. *'The Significance of Jewishness for Wittgenstein's Philosophy.'* In *Inquiry* Vol. 43, 383–401.

Stroll, Avrum. 1988. *Surfaces.* Minneapolis: University of Minnesota Press.

—. 1994. *Moore and Wittgenstein on Certainty.* New York: Oxford University Press.

—. 1998. *Sketches of Landscapes: Philosophy by Example.* Cambridge, Mass.: MIT Press.

—. 2000. *Twentieth Century Analytic Philosophy.* New York: Columbia University Press.

Szabados, Béla. 1999. *'Was Wittgenstein an Anti-Semite? The Significance of Anti-Semitism for Wittgenstein's Philosophy.'* Canadian Journal of Philosophy. Vol. 29, No. 1, 1–28.

Vendler, Zeno. 1995. 'Goethe, Wittgenstein, and the Essence of Color.' The Monist. Vol. 78, No. 4, 391–410.

von Wright, G. H. 1984. 'A Biographical Sketch'. In A Memoir by Norman Malcolm. New York: Oxford University Press, 1–20.

Wasserman, Gerhard D. 1990. 'Wittgenstein on Jews: Some Counter-Examples.' Philosophy. No. 65, 355–365.

Wittgenstein, Hermine. 1984. 'My Brother Ludwig.' In R. Rhees, ed., Recollections of Wittgenstein, 1–11, Oxford: Oxford University Press.

Wittgenstein, Ludwig. 1922. Tractatus Logico-Philosophicus. London: Routledge & Kegan Paul. New York: Oxford University Press.

—. 1958. Philosophical Investigations. Oxford: Blackwell.

—. 1960. The Blue and Brown Books. Oxford: Blackwell.

—. 1967. Letters from Ludwig Wittgenstein, with a Memoir. Paul Engelman. Oxford: Blackwell.

—. 1967. Zettel. Oxford: Blackwell.

—. 1969. On Certainty. Oxford: Blackwell.

—. 1980. Culture and Value. Oxford: Blackwell.

Wolgast, Elizabeth. 1977. Paradoxes of Knowledge. Ithaca: Cornell.

Index